T0148176

Anthony López
ablopez85@yahoo.com

Other books by Anthony López

"The Legacy Leader:
Leadership With A Purpose"
ISBN: 1-4107-3936-8

"Breakthrough Thinking:
The Legacy Leader's Role in Driving Innovation"
ISBN: 1-4208-3496-7

"The Leader's Lobotomy:
The Legacy Leader Avoids Promotion Induced Amnesia"
ISBN: 978-1-4398-1150-2

"The Leader In The Mirror:
The Legacy Leader's Critical Self-Assessment"
ISBN: 978-1-4670-2702

"See You At The Wake:
Healing Relationships before It's Too Late"
ISBN: 1-4184-1127-2

"Jag: Christian Lessons from My Golden Retriever"
ISBN: 978-1-4670-2694-9

The Legacy Leader as Superhero
LEGACYWOMAN

Anthony López

The Legacy Leader Series of Books

The Legacy Leader
Breakthrough Thinking
The Leader's Lobotomy
The Leader in the Mirror

authorHOUSE®

AuthorHouse™
1663 Liberty Drive
Bloomington, IN 47403
www.authorhouse.com
Phone: 1 (800) 839-8640

© *2018 Anthony López. All rights reserved.*

No part of this book may be reproduced, stored in a retrieval system, or transmitted by any means without the written permission of the author.

Published by AuthorHouse 01/19/2018

ISBN: 978-1-5462-2280-4 (sc)
ISBN: 978-1-5462-2278-1 (hc)
ISBN: 978-1-5462-2279-8 (e)

Library of Congress Control Number: 2017919746

Print information available on the last page.

Any people depicted in stock imagery provided by Thinkstock are models, and such images are being used for illustrative purposes only. Certain stock imagery © Thinkstock.

This book is printed on acid-free paper.

Because of the dynamic nature of the Internet, any web addresses or links contained in this book may have changed since publication and may no longer be valid. The views expressed in this work are solely those of the author and do not necessarily reflect the views of the publisher, and the publisher hereby disclaims any responsibility for them.

Contents

Dedication

*To my dad, Hector Luis Lopez, Sr. The best
father any man could pray for.*

*To my granddaughter, Madelyn Isabella Schneider. I pray that you
are inspired to grow-up to be the very best you that you can be.*

Advance Praise

"Tony has captured the fundamentals of leadership in a creative, practical and engaging way. No matter what stage of your leadership journey, this book will educate and entertain you at the same time."

Judith Garcia Galiana, Vice President
3M

"Once again Tony brings an inspirational gem to our hands. The pages go by quickly, and the book ends with you thirsty for more! Few people can bring leadership lessons to life with the ease that Lopez does!"

Ivan Tornos, WW President
Becton Dickinson

"No matter how long you've been a leader, Author Anthony Lopez's book will alter your current perceptions of leadership and cause you to be a become leader. I highly recommend it."

Dr. Shawne Duperon
Project Forgive Founder, Nobel Peace Prize Nominee

"With most books, we retain only a few pearls of wisdom. That's simply not the case with this one. After reading this book, all the leadership fundamentals of great leaders will forever be emblazoned in our brains."

Diana Bolivar, Principal
Diana Bolivar & Associates

"This book will not only change the way you think about leadership, but it will undoubtedly make you a better leader."

Dr. Laura Murillo, President & CEO
Houston Hispanic Chamber of Commerce

"Fun, memorable and fundamental all at the same time. After reading this book you will be a better leader. I totally recommend it."

Andrea Lisbona, CEO & Founder
Touchland

"Leaders, regardless of industry or whether they are novice or experienced in the art of leadership, will greatly benefit from this book."

Eric Guerin, Division Finance Vice President
Corning

"Simple, fun, and powerful. I dare you to read this book and forget the lessons in it. Lopez presents an innovative way to take the topic of leadership and cast it into new thinking with visuals never considered before. Fresh ideas for new generations in leadership roles."

Melanie Barstad, Member of Board of Directors
CINTAS

"I have read many books on leadership. None has captured my imagination more than this one. Tony brings leadership fundamentals to life in an artful and memorable way"

Thomas Draskovics, Chief Commercial Officer
SW Safety Solutions, Inc.

"Brilliant. In LegacyWoman, López presents leadership concepts and fundamentals in an unforgettable way."

Esther Aguilera, President & CEO
Latino Corporate Directors Association

"As a natural leader and talented executive, Anthony López inspires diverse teams every day. The leadership principles captured in LegacyWoman provides readers with resonating pillars to become better and stronger leaders themselves. A great and delightful read!"

Jocelyn Petersen, VP Finance
Ansell Healthcare

"Simple, fun, and powerful. A book on leadership for all generations."

Dr. Mitzi N. Morillo, Superintendent of Schools
Hunterdon County, NJ

"The cycle is complete! With this book, Lopez brings us full circle on a legacy leader's journey – from fundamentals and mechanics in his first book "The Legacy Leader: Leadership with a Purpose", to application of leadership principles in "Breakthrough thinking: The Legacy Leader's Role in Driving Innovation", to remembering lessons learned along the way in "The Leader's Lobotomy: The Legacy Leader Avoids Promotion Induced Amnesia", to conducting a critical self-assessment in "The Leader In the Mirror", to finally becoming a Superhero leader in this latest installment."

Thomas Savino, Chief Executive Officer
PROSPANICA

"I loved it. A leadership book that will resonate with people of all ages."

Jesse Penn, Retired Johnson & Johnson Executive

Acknowledgments

My leadership journey began nearly 35 years ago when I was an Air Force cadet, and I was completing my undergraduate studies. Since then, I have been blessed to be surrounded with great people, personally and professionally. Many have influenced my thinking and helped me become a better person. Some have had a profound influence on me, and have shaped me at a core level. I am grateful to all.

Over the past few years, as the content for this book was developing, I have worked with, and learned from, terrific professionals. I am grateful to colleagues from Ansell Healthcare, including Magnus Nicolin, Jocelyn Petersen, Angie Phillips, Mary DeSousa, Bill Reilly, Frederic Guyonneau, Chrystelle Fontan, David Lucas, Andrew Ng, Dan Barbour, Ilse Van Den Brent, Andrew Gilbert, Hasith Prematillake, and many others who made the journey at Ansell a fun discovery each day. I am especially grateful to Brenda J. Wilson, my executive assistant at Ansell, for simply making me better each day. Your support, friendship and prayers have strengthened me. To my Board of Director colleagues in PROSPANICA (formerly the National Society of Hispanic MBAs), thank you for allowing me to serve along-side with you, and lead such a great organization for a few years. I am grateful to Thomas Savino, Lino Carrillo, Larry Montes, Karen Flores, Julio Rocha, Carmen Heredia-Lopez, and Judith Garcia-Galiana for serving with me on the board. You are all strong leader role models for me, and for the organization.

No leader's journey can be made complete without the support and guidance of good friends to keep us grounded, and to provide a sounding board of good advice to help navigate the way. I count on a few great people to do that. Thank you Eric Guerin, Alton Stephens, Michael Khavinson, Jesse Penn, Ivan Tornos, and Curt Selquist.

Foreword

A simple Google search on the word 'leadership' yields more than eight-hundred million hits. Change the search to the word 'leader', and you get over one billion references to browse through! Even before recorded history, leadership - and more specifically - leaders have been talked about, studied, admired, feared, criticized, followed, sought after, respected, hated, built-up, and replaced. Some leaders have even been made immortal as their exploits and accomplishments – or failures – are captured in history books. One thing that has remained constant through the ages is our fascination with understanding leadership and leaders. Another is our need to have leaders that can inspire us all to fulfill our greatest potential both individually, and most certainly, collectively.

The volume of books and articles that have been written on leadership can easily fill the largest of libraries. The dimensions and complexities of leadership have been sliced and diced in every way imaginable. Thus, finding something new to be said about leadership, is rare. What is even more scarce yet, is finding a series of books that clearly, simply, and elegantly articulate the entire cycle of leadership as my friend Anthony López does in his Legacy Leader Series of Books. Beyond management theories, Tony's leadership book series captures what is often missed by standard biographies or M.B.A. case studies, the heart and spirit of a leader. In his books "The Legacy Leader" and "Breakthrough Thinking", Tony empowers us with practical and essential mechanics that set apart leaders who inspire, leave a legacy and make an impact greater than the title or responsibility they carry. Tony's next two books, "The Leader's Lobotomy" and "The Leader In The Mirror", provided a road map to further equip each of us as we develop in our own personal journey to become the best leaders we can be. Now, in "LegacyWoman and LegacyMan", he inspires us through an engaging and imaginative journey of self-discovery giving birth to the superhero inside each of us.

As a girl growing up in the eighties I was fascinated by the strength and resilience of television characters like wonder woman and the bionic woman. Their ability to remain strong, assertive, caring and beautiful all at once inspired me to grow up into a woman committed to make an impact while never losing the true essence of who I am along the way. Truth be told, we probably all secretly wanted to be one of them. Tony's playful use of our favorite superheroes to illustrate the most essential traits of leaders will be memorable for all who read this book. Gift wrapping the principles of leadership expressed here-in in a way that is fun – and even whimsical – is a brilliant approach to teach serious and important lessons that will make all of us better leaders.

I have known Tony for many years. I have had the blessing of working together to drive forward corporate movements, impact board rooms and bring to life what others saw as almost impossible. His tangible experience as a global leader has left a lasting impact not only on my own personal journey as a professional and now as an entrepreneur, but as a citizen of the world. He does not just write about leadership, he lives it. I know that he believes that great leaders are first and foremost men and women of great character and integrity. I can tell you that he is such a man. He believes that great leadership is about creating a legacy that our family, friends, and colleagues can be proud of. I can assure you that he has certainly created such a legacy for himself. But perhaps more importantly to him personally, is that he has helped me, and many others to build our legacy as we strive to apply the principles of what it takes to be a Legacy Leader. Honoring the journey and legacy of my mother, Diva Aurora Vargas de Gil, an executive who broke the glass ceiling for women in the oil industry in South America, I now proudly don the logo of LegacyWoman! Join me in the journey, and get ready to discover your full super-power.

Lili Gil Valletta

CEO & Co-Founder, CIEN+

ABOUT LILI GIL VALLETTA

Lili is a recognized cultural intelligence™ expert, World Economic Forum Young Global Leader and an award-winning entrepreneur. After a successful corporate career including a 10-year tenure at Johnson & Johnson, where she pioneered various diversity strategies, Lili cofounded CIEN+ and CulturIntel. Her firm offers big-data analytics, business and marketing strategies to leaders and corporations seeking to turn cultural trends and diversity into profits. Her methods of Cultural Intelligence™ and ability to use big data and AI tools to mine cultural insights, have been presented at numerous conferences, news outlets and universities like Princeton and Cornell, and been published by Harvard University. Lili is also the creator of the product innovation accelerator and masterclass tour Dreamers Ventures, empowering minority entrepreneurs with access to mentors, capital and opportunities, including the opportunity to launch on TV on HSN's American Dreams, where Lili is a guest host bringing inventors to market.

She is a regular TV commentator seen on Fox News, Fox Business and CNN en Español, and has been featured by Forbes, The Huffington Post, CNN

Money, The NY Daily News, MM&M, among others. Lili serves as a board member of the Harvard Women's Leadership Board, National Board of Directors of the YMCA USA, mentor to the Stanford Latino Entrepreneur Leaders Program and member of the New York State Council on Women and Girls. She holds a degree in Business Administration from Southwestern

Adventist University, and M.B.A. from the University of Colorado and an executive degree from the Harvard Kennedy School in Global Leadership and Public Policy. She lives in New York City with her husband, entrepreneur and former NFL player Chris Valletta and her two sons.

Preface

"Faster than a speeding bullet. More powerful than a locomotive. Able to leap tall buildings in a single bound. Look! Up in the sky! It's a bird. It's a plane. It's Superman! Yes, it's Superman-strange visitor from another planet who came to Earth with powers and abilities far beyond those of mortal men. Superman-who can change the course of mighty rivers, bend steel with his bare hands, and who, disguised as Clark Kent, mild mannered reporter for a great metropolitan newspaper, fights the never-ending battle for Truth, Justice and the American Way."

From 1952 to 1957, the syndicated television program Superman opened with these words. The show captured the imagination of people of all ages. I remember watching the show in the 1970s when I was a young boy. I had a special towel that I wore around my neck as a cape while I was glued to the black and white television. No doubt, every little boy wanted to be

Superman. That is, until a dark and mysterious character came into the scene named Batman. He had all the cool gadgets! Of course, it did not hurt that he was a millionaire as well. Clark Kent was only a reporter for the Daily Planet. Thus, Batman became "the guy to be".

Since the debut of Superman in 1938, stories of superheroes have become a part of, and dominated American folklore. As in the case of Superman, Batman and Spiderman, to name just a few, some superheroes have had adventures that have lasted generations. Brought to life first in American comic books, these characters have crossed over into all forms of media including television and movies. They have evolved – mutated – in some cases to accommodate our changing demographics to be inclusive of women super heroines and diverse "heroes of color".

Everyone has a favorite superhero. We each have one superhero with whom we connect more than any of the others; that one superhero that we secretly wish we could be. We wonder what it would be like if we had their powers, and we imagine what we could do if we could be them even for a brief time. Why do superheroes inspire us the way they do? Is it that they have an incredible way of always being at the right place at the right time? Or maybe it's that they always win in the end. Who doesn't like a happy ending when the good guys win, the bad guys get punished and life seems to be in order again?

As children, we look up to superheroes. We admire them and we trust them. We follow their advice and would gladly follow them into battle against the bad guys. We root for them when they are in the middle of a fight. When they feel bad, we feel bad. When they feel good, we feel good. When superheroes let us down we are very disappointed, but we forgive them when they make a mistake because we know that in the end they will always do what is right. We like the fact that superheroes always help the helpless and are selfless in their endeavors. We admire their courage and appreciate them for putting themselves in harm's way to save people. Our superheroes are not perfect. They always have a fault or weakness that some of their arch enemies try to exploit; but our superheroes don't let that defeat them. Instead they persevere and overcome their weaknesses to ultimately defeat the bad guys, and restore order where chaos reigned before.

Superheroes don't exist in the real world. The closest that we can come to having superheroes in our world are teachers who nurture us through our formative years, and nurses and doctors who care for us when we are ill. We look at firefighters and police officers, and hail them as heroes because they work tirelessly to keep us safe. We reserve the highest honor – the Medal of Honor – for the service men and women who selflessly fight for our country, and even lay down their life if necessary, to preserve our way of life. Those are superheroes in my book.

Maybe – just maybe – the leaders we choose to follow can also achieve superhero status in our world. Just like the fictional superheroes, ideally, we look up to our leaders. We want to admire and trust them. We are willing to follow them into battle. We want to be connected to our leaders, rooting for them when they are in the middle of a fight. We want to follow leaders who possess great courage, are honest, and who have our best interests at heart. We want humble, yet strong leaders who fight for what is right. We accept that our leaders are not perfect, and we are willing to forgive them when they make a mistake if they deal with it transparently and with dignity and respect. We also know that our leaders have weaknesses.

These weaknesses can even endear the leader to us if they deal with them directly with humility and honesty.

By definition, a superhero has superhuman powers. However, some of the most popular superheroes, such as Batman, are without such powers. Batman is an ordinary human being who does extraordinary things. This is what we need in our leaders; we need them to be ordinary people who do extraordinary things. More importantly, we need leaders to be people who inspire others to achieve extraordinary, superhero-like accomplishments. The best leaders strive to accomplish what no other superhero ever has; they create an army of superheroes who when properly aligned, directed and motivated achieve feats that not even Superman could fathom.

In the fictional world of comic books there are hundreds of superheroes. Their skills and special powers are limited only by their creator's imagination. The ideal superhero would be one that combines the best qualities of all the characters, and is not susceptible to the inherent flaws or weaknesses that each of the superhero has. But even in the imaginary world that's simply not reality! All superheroes have strengths and they have weaknesses. The same is true of all leaders. In this book, we will explore the traits of some of the most popular superheroes and draw analogies to lessons learned from these as they relate to leadership qualities we want our leaders to exhibit.

Since their introduction in the 1930s, superheroes of all kinds have been created. Their skills are as diverse as the costumes they wear. They each have a singular source of strength. Their personal styles and their weaknesses are uniquely their own. Historically, until the 1960s, superheroes conformed to the American standard of "leading-man hero" popular of the first half of the 20th century. Most of them were white, middle to upper class, heterosexual, professional men. Fortunately, in the decades that have followed minority superheroes have been created to include strong female characters and non-Caucasian men. Superheroes such as Wonder Woman, Batwoman, Catwoman, and Storm are as popular today as their male counterparts. In the late 1960s, superheroes of other racial groups began to appear. The Black Panther was the first serious black superhero followed in the early 1980s with the first non-Caucasian Green Lantern.

Despite their uniqueness and individuality, superheroes all have some common traits. A strong moral compass, extraordinary skills, a strong sense of responsibility, and a willingness to put themselves at risk for the benefit of others, are a few of the characteristics we love about superheroes. It is these kind of common traits, that link all superheroes toward the achievement of one common goal: the betterment of mankind. Likewise, the best leaders all share some common qualities. In this book, we look at the traits shared by superheroes and learn how they can be applied to ensure that our leaders are the most effective men and women with one common goal: to create a better world and leave a legacy that we can all be proud of.

This is the fifth book in the Legacy Leader series. The first – "The Legacy Leader – began with my thesis that of all the traits a leader demonstrates, only two are non-negotiable: character and integrity. All other qualities and skills necessary for effective leadership can be acquired via education, experience, and especially the school of hard-knocks. Character and integrity however, are woven into the very fabric of our DNA make-up and are non-negotiable.

Once character and integrity are compromised, it results in a leader's failure in reaching the maximum level of effectiveness had their character and integrity been kept whole. "The Legacy Leader" also addressed what can be labeled as the mechanics of leadership. It presented the most fundamental qualities and behaviors that leaders can and must exhibit if they are to build "Achieving Organizations" with a personal legacy of which they can be proud.

The second book in the 'The Legacy Leader Series' is "Breakthrough Thinking: The Legacy Leader's Role In Driving Innovation." It addressed what the Legacy Leader must do to drive teams and organizations to accomplish things they would have initially thought impossible.

In the third volume, "The Leader's Lobotomy", we pricked the memories of leaders who, having reached positions of significant responsibility in their organizations, suddenly, and without warning, develop PIA – Promotion Induced Amnesia. In this fictional short story, we used a bit of humor to address a subject of profound significance: the leader's need to ensure that he or she practice the most fundamental and important elements of leadership. We introduced the main characters of Jim, a recently promoted executive, and Ted, his Corporate Guardian Angel. The story walked us through a year in Jim's life as a new executive, and how Ted coached him on important leadership fundamentals to ensure that Jim avoided suffering from Promotion Induced Amnesia.

In "The Leader in The Mirror", Ted, back by popular demand, comes back into Jim's life. The story picks-up eight years later. Jim has been promoted to President of the company, and Ted will help him take a hard look in the mirror. Leaders must be willing to do a critical self-assessment, being honest with themselves about their strengths and weaknesses. The leader's journey is one of self-discovery and growth; and sometimes it takes looking sternly in the mirror, even if we don't like what we see.

In "LegacyWoman" we continue the journey of the Legacy Leader, learning and applying important lessons to continuously improve on our performance as leaders. We don't expect our leaders to be invincible or immortal. We certainly don't expect them to wear spandex uniforms or masks. However, we do want them to exhibit superhero-like qualities. We want leaders to be individuals we can admire and who can inspire us to achieve greatness.

CHAPTER 1

The Birth of LegacyWoman & LegacyMan

Our fascination with Superheroes can be traced back for centuries. Before we had cape crusaders and super-human strength characters who defied our known laws of physics, we had Samson. First described in the Bible in the book of Judges, chapters thirteen though sixteen, this Bible character's exploits also appear in Josephus's Antiquities of the Jews, written in the last decade of the 1st Century AD.

Samson, a man endowed with Herculean qualities is granted superhuman strength by God to combat his enemies. He performs heroic feats that no other mortal man could. He wrestled lions and defeated an entire army of men with a donkey's jawbone as his only weapon. Like every superhero, Samson had a great weakness. In his case it was Delilah. She had been bribed by Samson's enemies to discover the secret to his strength: he had made a pledge to God to never cut his hair. Eventually Delilah convinces Samson to reveal his secret, and while he is sleeping, she cuts his hair causing Sampson to lose his strength, and thus to be captured by his enemies. The story does not end there! Samson's hair grows back and his strength returns, and he once again defeats his enemies.

Samson's escapades and adventures are nothing short of spectacular. It's the thing that movies are made of. Historical accounts of his life include all intrigue and excitement of the greatest of Hollywood epic films. What little boy, upon hearing the stories of Samson would not want to be him? No doubt before kids played Superman, Batman or Spiderman, they played being Samson.

From the beginning of time we have always looked to heroes to inspire us. Children of all generations have had characters, some fictional and some real, that they looked to as role models. These were the characters that in many ways shaped our thinking; we wanted to be like them! This is certainly not a new idea. The geeks of today have Einstein, Edison and Bill Gates as their heroes; whereas the geeks of the seventeen-century had Sir Isaac Newton and Galileo that they wanted to be like. No doubt for a hundred years after George Washington led our army to victory, every little boy who played "war" wanted to be the General. Eventually Washington was replaced by other notorious military leaders of the day. It seems our evolving needs create the foundation of the kinds of superheroes we need in our lives.

In the 1930s superheroes as we know them today came into vogue. The first superheroes in fact were ordinary humans who were doing extraordinary things. Characters such as Dick Tracy and The Shadow, who despite the wonderful gadgets they had, were still ordinary people. It wasn't until Superman was introduced in June 1938 that we had characters with powers beyond those of normal humans. Since then there have been hundreds of characters created, all with their own set of special skills, strengths, and weaknesses. There is, it seems, a superhero to meet all taste and styles. For instance, in the early days, while Superman was portrayed as pure and clean, Batman on the other hand was a rough character who saw fighting as a means to an end. Although he did not have superhero powers, he did have a high intellect, a cool costume, and neat gadgets that would put him on par with the other superheroes. The list of characters grew as quickly as the publishers could create stories to print about them.

The Flash, the Human Torch, the Shield, Captain America, Wonder Woman, the Green Lantern, Catwoman, SuperGirl, Wolverine, Thor, Aquaman, and the forever popular Spiderman are but a few of the characters that helped create a complete virtual universe. Out of the hundreds of superhero characters, some stand out as the most historically significant: Superman, Batman, Wonder Woman, Spiderman, and Captain America are among them. Each of these, perhaps more than any of the others, captured our imaginations and influenced our thinking. The lessons we learned from these superhero characters as we grew up reading about them in comic books, listening to them on the radio, or watching them in television programs and films, certainly have impacted generations of people.

We look to Superman because he always does the right thing and behaves ethically in all circumstances. We want to be like him. We love Batman, because he has a dark side to him that causes him at times to "cross-the-line". However, he always does it to beat the bad guy in the name of justice. We root for him because deep-down we want the bad-guy to "get his". We all wish we had Wonder Woman's truth lasso so that we can know what people are really thinking and not only what they are saying – especially our politicians! We love Spiderman because he's the quintessential unpopular geek and weakling who becomes the cool superhero that every girl wants to date. Whatever the reasons, we look to superheroes to be our role models and to teach us right from wrong. Each of these characters fills a special need in our society to ensure that our way of life is protected from those who would want to undermine it and do us harm.

In our society today, we need a new brand of superhero. One who will embody the best of the best from other great superheroes and to whom we can look-up to, trust and admire. We don't need another fictional character that can magically overcome the laws of physics. It's not a man or woman who can bend steel with their bare hands that we need; but rather we need a man or woman who can help create industries that can bend steel to make what we need. It's not a man or woman with a magical string that causes people to tell the truth that we need; rather, we need men and women who will tell the truth when they lead. It's not a man or woman who can fly around the world that we need; rather we need a man or woman who can unite people around the world in one common goal to achieve a greater good. It's not a man or woman that is fast enough to avoid bullets and arrows shot at them that we need; rather we need men and women who are willing to take those bullets and arrows shot at the people that they lead. It's not a man or woman who uses a costume to hide their true-identity that we need; rather we need a man or woman of great character and integrity willing to be humbly exposed as they lead. We need LegacyMan. We need LegacyWoman.

LegacyMan and LegacyWoman are not superheroes in the pure definition of the word. They do not have special super human powers. They cannot violate the laws of physics and fly under their own power. Bullets don't bounce off LegacyMan. He's mortal. He's fallible. As we will discover in this book, LegacyMan and LegacyWoman embody the best qualities of all the best superheroes and channel all their energies towards one pursuit: to lead in a way that creates a legacy that we can all be proud of.

One important difference between LegacyWoman and all other fictional superheroes is this: there can only be one Superman, Batman, or Spiderman. In the real-world there can be many LegacyMen and LegacyWomen. We don't have to be born in planet Krypton to have our "superpowers". We don't need to be bitten by a radioactive spider to mutate into a powerful spider web swinging crime fighter. We don't even need to be a billionaire, with an anger management riddled alter ego and cool gadgets, to defeat our enemies. What we need to be a LegacyMan or a LegacyWoman, we can learn. We can learn from reading about other great LegacyMen and LegacyWomen, observing them, and most importantly, from practicing their leadership principles. Like other superheroes however, LegacyMan has some inherent weaknesses. Also like other superheroes, it is these weaknesses that usually cause their downfall. Thus, we must learn what these are, and do everything possible to avoid them. For simplicity throughout this book we will use LegacyMan and LegacyWoman interchangeably. It is certainly true that great leadership has nothing to do with the gender of the leader, but the content of their character, and all the other traits we will speak of in the coming chapters.

Let the journey begin. The signal has been given. The world needs LegacyWomen and LegacyMen in all areas of business, private and public sectors to step-up and lead. Up, up and away!

CHAPTER 2
The Making of a Superhero

Most superheroes share some common traits that endear them to their loyal followers and admirers. No doubt every character is unique and especially equipped with his or her own set of special talents. One other commonality among superheroes is that they each have an "Achilles heel". Sometimes they have more than one!

Achilles was a superhero of sorts. In Greek mythology, Achilles was a hero of the Trojan War and the greatest warrior of Homer's Iliad. He is described as strong, powerful and very handsome. Legends state that Achilles' body was invulnerable except for his heels. After he died due to a poisoned arrow shot by Paris into his heel, Achilles' heel has come to mean a person's principle weaknesses. It seems ironic that the weakness of a superhero-like character has come to symbolize the major flaws in all of us. Thus, as we consider the common traits shared by superheroes, we must also consider the common vulnerabilities.

There are six common traits shared by superheroes. Let's look at them individually:

A strong moral compass

In modern days, a compass seems almost like an obsolete instrument. Perhaps better stated, it's an instrument that we take for granted. Before the advent of modern day navigators built into our vehicles, before cellular telephones were common-place, and long before we had global positioning systems (GPS), sailors and explorers relied on a very basic device called a compass. It is based on a very simple concept: with its northward facing needle, it is a consistent and true indicator of physical direction.

By placing the word "moral" in front of "compass" we evoke a different picture and add a new dimension to the "direction" we choose to travel. A moral compass is a reference to a person's direction in life and the processes that they follow as they live their lives. The concept of morality is also fundamentally simple. It essentially comes down to conduct that is either right or wrong. It is behavior that is wrapped-up within the basic character, integrity, and ethics of the person. Clearly the only question is: who defines morality? After all, one person's moral compass may point in a different direction from someone else's'. One thing is certain however, there are some universally accepted moral absolutes, and it is these that superheroes always adhere to. These standards are defined by our society standards even more so than the laws by which we are governed.

Importantly, there is no GPS for moral conduct. There is no machine that measures our moral direction and provides us course corrections when we are off-course. Superman does not need a GPS to let him know the difference between what is right and wrong. He follows his internal moral compass for that.

Like all superheroes, LegacyMan must adhere to a strict code of conduct and always ensure that their moral compass is pointing in the right direction.

A Sense of Responsibility

In doing research for this book, I considered the meaning of the word "responsibility", and its origins. Responsibility means to have a duty to deal with something or having control over someone. It implies authority, control power, and even leadership at times. It can also imply being to blame for something. The Spanish word "deber" may also give some insight into the concept of responsibility. It means to "owe". Its expanded meaning is to "owe it to oneself" or to "owe to others". A few questions we might ask are: where does that sense of responsibility come from? Why is that sense of responsibility and duty stronger in some people than others?

Those are very good questions, and we should all take an introspective look at ourselves as we answer them. The bottom line is this: a strong sense of responsibility really means having a strong moral code and includes the willingness to risk one's own safety and well-being in pursuit of the greater good without the expectation of reward or personal gain.

Superheroes never expect to gain personally as they go about saving mankind on a routine basis. In fact, they often shun the limelight and fame that naturally comes with their incredible feats; opting instead to remain obscure and even unknown to their adoring fans. With true superheroes it's never about "them". They remain humble and always have a servant heart, only desiring to do what is right and in the best interest of those around them. LegacyWoman take note! That's what we need you to be like.

Extraordinary Powers and Abilities

Superhero powers vary tremendously from one character to the next. Often their powers include the ability to fly along with some enhanced sensory perception. This typically includes Hawkeye-like vision, a supernatural hearing ability, and even the projection of lighting-like bolts of energy, are not unusual among superheroes. There are some superheroes, such as Batman, that possess no superhuman powers. Instead

Batman relies on his advanced martial arts skills and advanced intellect to accomplish his incredible feats.

The Flash uses his speed to overwhelm his adversary. Spiderman's web and his ability to crawl up the side of buildings, not to mention his heightened senses, make his nemesis shiver with fear. Wolverine's regenerative abilities to heal himself after he has been wounded frustrate his enemies and Thor's mighty hammer causes his opponents to hide for cover. Whatever their powers and skills, one thing is certain: these superheroes have fine-tuned their special abilities and have learned to use them to their fullest advantage.

The same has to be true with LegacyMan. He must learn what his extraordinary powers and skills are, and then go about leveraging them fully to help him achieve his objectives.

Access to Technology or Resources

Some superheroes have all the cool toys. Iron Man's powered armor suits, Green Lantern's power ring, along with Wonder Woman's lasso of truth, and Wolverine's adamantium claws are just a few of the gadgets we all wish we could have at our disposal. Captain America's vibranium-iron disk shape shield is the envy of every superhero in his neighborhood. But without a doubt, the superhero with the coolest gadgets is Batman.

Batman's utility belt is made of a Kevlar strap and metal buckle. It houses an array of endless tools including high tension wires to help him fly across open spaces from one building to another. The buckle itself contains a miniature camera and a radio (yes, radio was cool and novel at one point in history). No matter what trouble he seems to find himself in, he can always reach for his utility belt. MacGyver has nothing on Batman! Batman also has access to other sophisticated technology including the batmobile and the batplane. He keeps these impressive toys in his batcave, where he also has access to a laboratory complete with the computers and equipment that he needs to do all sorts of forensic analysis. Batman is definitely the gadget superhero. Fortunately for him, he is also independently wealthy so he can fund his incredibly expensive taste in toys.

When it comes to resources, superheroes do what they must to ensure they have the tools to get the job done. This must also be true for LegacyWoman. She must ensure that she makes the necessary investment so that she, and her organization, have access to whatever is needed to achieve the objectives.

A Personal Theme

Each superhero has a personal theme that is uniquely their own. It's their own personal brand and they are consistently faithful to that brand. Whether it's their uniform, or the special names they use for their gadgets (e.g. batmobile, batcave), superheroes are identified with these.

Other factors that determine a superheroes' personal theme is their character. Do they have a sense of humor? Are they high strung and very serious or are they more playful in their approach? It's their style, both when they are in superhero mode as well as when they are in "disguise", that also defines who they are. Finally, their motivation also determines their personal theme. In the case of Spiderman, it's his sense of responsibility that motivates him. Wonder Woman feels a formal calling to do what she does. Batman was first motivated by a vendetta against criminals, and Superman is driven by a strong belief in justice and humanitarian service.

LegacyMan will also have a personal theme. It will be important that they determine what that theme will be, and how they will behave consistently over time to build their personal brand and use it effectively to achieve their objectives.

Courage

If there is one trait all superheroes – fictional and real – have, it is courage. We all marvel at the special effects of today's movies portraying superheroes taking on the villains. These evil characters also exhibit super-powers, or have all sorts of weaponry at their disposal. I suppose for cinematographic dramatic effect, the villain typically first appears to be beating the hero, sometimes bringing them to the edge of death itself. However, our superhero does not quit, they adapt, recover, and figure out a way to defeat the bad guy, saving the day and making the world safe once again.

This is not very different from what real superheroes – LegacyMen and LegacyWomen – often face. They encounter challenges, and defeat problems that to us ordinary folks, can seem like monsters. The point is, they must have the courage to take on the scary things, be willing to take a beating in the process, and never think about quitting until the mission is complete. That's the courage a Legacy Leader must exhibit if they want to inspire their people to follow their lead.

These six common superhero traits help to create a strong base from which we can build. All levity aside, the point of this chapter is simply to establish the need for leaders to be people who share some important core principles. We want and need leaders who have a strong moral compass and behave according to an ethical code of conduct. We want our leaders to be men and women with a strong sense of responsibility, who put the interest of their followers and those they serve ahead of their own. We want leaders to develop and use their extraordinary skills and abilities to inspire those around them to achieve great results. We expect our leaders to use all resources available to them to lead the creation of innovative new solutions to many of the societal and technological challenges we face. Finally we need leaders who will be true to their own personal theme; individuals who say what they do and do what they say.

In the coming chapters, we will take a look at a few of our favorite superheroes, and learn some important leadership lessons from each of them. In each chapter, we begin with a short biography on the character – mostly for the geeks like me who live part-time in the fictional world of superheroes; but also because it helps inform our understanding of the superhero and why they behave the way they do. Let the journey continue.

CHAPTER 3

Superman
Visionary & Ethical

The man of steel. That is Superman's nickname. Ever since the character was introduced in 1933 by Jerry Siegeland and Joe Shuster, Superman has been flying high above Metropolis, keeping it safe from all sorts of bad actors. I suppose there are few people in the world not familiar with this extraterrestrial who landed on earth in a small space craft. He had been launched in a spaceship by his parents to escape Krypton just before the planet exploded.

Superman possesses many powers including: flight, superhuman strength, cold breath, super-speed, enhanced hearing, all of which make him nearly indestructible by human standards. There is one special power, and two character traits, that more than any of Superman's special powers and qualities that LegacyMan must emulate first and foremost: Superman's x-ray vision and his uncompromising commitment to ethics.

X-Ray Vision

Superman's x-ray vision provides him an ability to see through physical objects. Though called x-ray vision, this power has little to do with the actual effect of "real x-rays". Rather than get hung-up on the science of x-rays, we should focus on what this "special vision" allows Superman to do. He is able to selectively see through objects or barriers as though they are translucent or invisible. This allows Superman to have an insight that those around him do not. He can see the bad guys hiding behind walls before they can see him. This insight allows Superman to effectively deal with the situation. LegacyMan needs to have his own form of "x-ray" vision. LegacyMan's vision should allow him to see past barriers that might get in the way. In fact, LegacyMan's vision looks well past objects and barriers and sees through them as though they are translucent and don't even exist. It's a vision that provides insight and indicates a direction or course of action.

Even Superman's vision can be limited: he is unable to see through lead. Lex Luthor, Superman's archenemy, took full advantage of this weakness when he hid kryptonite in a lead box so that Superman could not see the danger that awaited him when he opened it. The fact that Superman's vision was limited or impaired by the lead box almost caused his death! LegacyMan needs to learn from Superman's experience. Not having vision can be lethal. Before moving forward, and venturing into the unknown, LegacyMan must remember to have a vision that will protect him and his followers from potential doom.

Commitment to Ethics

In Alan Axelrod's book "Office Superman" he writes this:

> *"Ethics is at the core of the Superman chronicles. This much seems too self-evident even to discuss. From the very beginning, Superman dedicates himself to serving*

truth, justice, and whatever is right, as well as defending
the weak against the tyranny and terror of the strong."

He goes on to write:

*"We read Superman's adventures knowing full well that, if he chose,
the man of steel's superpower could give him anything the world
has to offer. He could become a master thief or a supreme tyrant.
He could become the world's richest man, if he wanted to, without
ever having to take a particularly immoral, let along evil course."*

Superman acts ethically; but even for him it's not always easy
to do. In its simplest definition, to act ethically means to discern
between what is right and what is wrong, and then to do what
is right. That is often easier said than done. With the incredible
powers that Superman possesses he certainly could have taken
the much easier and selfish path, and use his powers for his
own personal gain. Yet he chose to dedicate himself instead to
doing what is right, even if it was not always in his personal
best interest. LegacyWoman must emulate Superman in this
way. She must always do what is right and she must always
be more interested in serving other's interest before her own.

There are six basic principles when it comes to ethics:

1. Ethics is not always easy.
2. Ethics may negatively impact your bottom line.
3. Ethical decisions are based on reliable data and facts.
4. Ethical decisions always consider the long-term impact.
5. Ethical decisions may sacrifice short-term objectives.
6. Ethical decisions consider the needs of everyone affected.

Considering these non-negotiable ethics principles needs to be part of LegacyMan's decision making process. Before taking action, he must take into account the impact of his decisions on his colleagues, subordinates, customers, shareholders, and the community-at-large. He cannot afford to make decisions in a vacuum or only thinking of the short-term benefits of his decided course of action. There are a few simple steps that LegacyMan can take to help him make consistent ethical decisions. They are:

"Wear and walk in someone else's sandals"

"Walk a mile in my shoes, and you will only then understand me better." This statement rings very true. By this we simply mean, think about an issue from another's point of view before making and implementing a decision regarding that issue. Sometimes the hardest thing for a leader to do, is to do nothing. It's even hard to simply slow down before taking action. Yet there are occasions when that is exactly what they should do. Pause long enough to make sure they have heard all the appropriate perspectives and opinions that help inform their decisions. Often, it's not until we have placed ourselves – in as much as it is possible – in someone else's position, that we can understand their perspective. LegacyWoman knows how important this is, and she takes the time to truly listen and understand. This does not mean that she needs to have perfect and one-hundred percent complete information before moving forward. Waiting for that can be even more damaging than not first understanding and listening for other's ideas. There's a fine balance that the leader must learn to navigate between moving too fast, and standing still waiting for data.

A few years ago, while I was in an executive leadership team meeting with the company I was employed by at the time, we were debating an approach to a decision we were wrestling with. I was pushing for faster action. After a few minutes of discussing the issue, the boss said "I learned some time ago not to make a decision until I had to, but when I had to, make it quickly". I understood his point. I was arguing for a decision to be made before it was really necessary to make at that very moment. I backed off, and it turns out, he was right. He usually was.

Assess collateral damage

One of my favorite Star Trek characters is Spock, the Vulcan first officer to Captain James T. Kirk. In one of the most dramatic scenes in the movie the Wrath of Khan, Spock transfers his *katra*—his memories and experience—to Dr. McCoy, and then sacrifices himself to save the ship and its crew. Before he dies, in a dramatic and touching scene he comforts Kirk, his long-time friend, explaining that his decision to sacrifice himself was logical. He expressed it this way: "the needs of the many outweigh the needs of the few or the one". Spock assessed the potential collateral damage to his crew, his friends, his ship, and even the "Federation of Planets" as he made his decision. LegacyMan and LegacyWoman know this for sure: you always put the needs of your followers first, and they always behave in ways that looks after the greater good of their team, organization, company, and community. They never worry about their own self-interest. That is because they instinctively know that if they care for their people, their people will take care of accomplishing the mission, which in the end is the leader's responsibility.

Be accountable to the decisions made

U.S. president Harry S. Truman had a sign with the inscription "the buck stops here" on his desk. Truman didn't originate the phrase, but Fred M. Canfil, United States Marshal for the Western District of Missouri and a Truman friend arranged for a copy of it to be made and sent to him. Truman proudly displayed the sign on his desk throughout his presidency. His message was clear: He accepted personal responsibility for the way the country was governed.

LegacyMan understands that they must always do what they know to be right. They must consider the impact of their decisions on others, and ultimately, they take complete accountability for their decisions. Finally, LegacyMan understands that ethics defines their character. Axelrod puts it like this:

> *"Consistently ethical decisions are difficult – perhaps impossible – to make in the absence of character and yet it is by means of consistently ethical decisions that character is both developed and demonstrated."*

The eternal debate: Is a leader born or made?

There is one final and interesting leadership lesson we can take from Superman; or perhaps it's more from his earthly parents, Martha and Johnathan Kent. We often debate whether a leader is born or made. It certainly is a fun discussion to have, although it's real impact to the effectiveness of a leader is not important. After, all, why do we really care if a leader is born or made? What we really care about is who they are as leaders and what they do. Nevertheless, we are intrigued by the debate. So, what's the correct answer? It seems, it's a bit of both. Leaders are certainly born with certain qualities and traits that are inherent in their DNA. However, how they are raised, and what they are taught, no doubt influences who they become as men and women. In my estimation, this last point is supremely more important.

Johnathan and Martha Kent, are the adoptive parents of Superman. When they found him as a baby in the wreckage of his crashed space ship, they took him as their own and raised him in the rural town of Smallville, Kansas. The Kents are usually portrayed as caring parents who instilled in Clark a strong work ethic, of a very strong moral code. In fact, they encourage Clark to use his powers for the betterment of humanity! We should be glad that this extraterrestrial was not found by a criminal-minded family bent on doing harm rather than good. Instead of having a Superman, we would have had a Supervillain. Clearly the influence of his parents was key to how Clark Kent, a.k.a. Superman, would behave his entire life. They had no control over what his powers are, but they certainly controlled how he used them by teaching him the difference between right and wrong. Leaders may be born with some special qualities about them, but absent the proper teaching, mentoring, and coaching, they will never likely realize the full potential of their powers.

CHAPTER 4

Wonder Woman
Truthful & Credible

Wonder Woman is a formidable character. She's intelligent, has superhuman strength, she has access to magical weaponry, and is a skilled hand-to-hand and weapons combat specialist. Indeed, Princess Diana has a powerful arsenal of weapons at her disposal. However, none are more connected to Wonder Woman than her indestructible bracelets and her Lasso of Truth. Her bracelets, formed from the remnants of the Aegis (Zeus' shield) are able to absorb the impact of bullets from automatic weapons and deflect energy blasts. Without doubt however, her most unique weapon as a superhero is her Lasso of Truth. The Lasso of Truth forces anyone held by it to tell the truth without exception. That's real power!

For as long as man has existed, the quest for the perfect "lie detector" has been on-going. All sorts of ancient methodologies have been used by civilizations dating back thousands of years to detect when someone was telling the truth and when they were telling a lie. By the late 1800s measuring devices had been invented that measured changes in a person's blood pressure while they were being interrogated to determine if they were telling the truth. Since then devices have been developed to measure breathing, muscular activity and other psychological changes to get after the truth. Today, the modern-day polygraph is a part of almost every major investigation, and it's even widely used in job interviewing processes before a person is hired by a company.

Why is getting at the truth so important? Why do we work so hard to get at the truth? In criminal cases, the answer is obvious. We want to make sure we have the facts correct before risking convicting someone who is innocent. The simple answer as to why we fervently seek the truth is this: we search for the truth because we loathe deception.

Even the word deception connotes things we don't like. Words such as deceit, bluff, half-truths and concealment come to mind when we think of deception. In many cases, it is quite difficult to know when we are being deceived. Through propaganda or outright lies, we can be fooled into believing something that is not true. Sometimes we can be manipulated into taking a course of action we would not have chosen had we known the truth. Deception is never done by accident. When we are deceived it's because someone chose carefully to spin a story or present data as fact that may be false. When we are deceived, we feel victimized and taken advantage of. That's why we want the truth so badly; because no one wants to be deceived.

When it comes to leadership, a primary reason that the truth is important is because of its direct relationship to credibility; and credibility is one of the non-negotiable foundations of great leadership.

In their book "The Leadership Challenge" Kouzes and Posner have this to say about credibility:

> "Honest, forward-looking, inspiring and competent: these are
> the characteristics that have remained constant over more

than twenty years of economic growth and recession, the surge in new technology enterprises, the birth of the World Wide Web, the further globalization of business and industry, the ever-changing political environment, and the expansion, bursting, and regeneration of the Internet economy. The relative importance of the most desired qualities had varied somewhat over time, but there has been no change in the fact that these are the four qualities people want most in their leaders. Whether they believe their leaders are true to these values is another matter, but what they would like from these has remained constant. This list of four consistent findings is useful in and of itself – but there's a more profound implication revealed by our research. Three of these four key characteristics make up what communication experts refer to as the source of credibility."

Kouzes and Posner go on to conclude that "credibility is the foundation of leadership". Personal credibility starts with having a reputation of being honest and always telling the truth. Building credibility requires hard work. It can take time. To gain credibility a leader must demonstrate behaviors that, sustained over prolonged periods, create an impression with the people they lead that they can trust the leader. As I described in my book "The Legacy Leader", to build credibility a leader must engage in the following daily actions:

1. Communicate a clear vision
2. Engage followers in the vision
3. Motivate their followers
4. Behave in ways consistent with the vision
5. Be where the action is
6. Be accountable for behaviors and results

The leader who goes about these actions daily has the best chance of building their credibility with the team. The bad news is this: it only takes one lie to destroy the leader's credibility. One lie! That's the power of deception. Fortunately, the truth is an even more powerful weapon in the leader's arsenal. LegacyWoman must understand this universal principle about leadership: they must always tell the truth.

It is important that we take a moment to highlight the difference between miscommunication and deception. The key to deception is intent. If there is intent to mislead or hide information, then we consider it deception. However, leaders must be aware that they may be perceived as being deceptive if information they communicate is inaccurate or incomplete. A leader may do a lousy job of communicating information and therefore create a problem of miscommunication that is not based on a lie. The damage to their credibility, albeit temporary, may have already been done because of the miscommunication. How the leader recovers from this will be based on two factors: first, it becomes clear that the leader was indeed not being dishonest in their communication. Second, how quickly the leader corrects the information. All leaders may from time to time have a problem with communicating something that is not quite complete or accurate. No one is perfect. Of course, leaders need to work hard to minimize these occurrences. However, more important than minimizing the opportunities for being misinterpreted or for communicating incomplete or inaccurate information, is dealing with them quickly and honestly.

In their essay "The Puzzles of Leadership" published in the Druker Foundation's "The Leader of The Future", Anthony Smith and Steven M. Bornstein define the Six C's of Leadership Credibility. They write:

"The research on credibility suggest that when one individual attempts to influence another, the potential follower engages in both conscious and unconscious evaluation of the potential leader and will follow, striving to perform at his or her full potential, only the leader deemed to be credible. Credibility is based on six criteria that we call the Six Cs of Leadership Credibility:

1. *Conviction*

2. *Character*

3. *Care*

4. *Courage*

5. *Composure*

6. *Competence"*

Clearly, to be successful leaders they must be able to influence their followers. The degree to which they can do this depends entirely on their level of credibility, and their credibility comes directly from the behaviors described by Bornstein and Smith, along with the ones just described before that. The underpinning of these behaviors, however is being honest and truthful. Regardless of the level of conviction, passion and commitment that a leader has for his or her vision, if they are not seen as truthful, they will fail. A leader who demonstrates care and concern for his or her followers will be perceived as disingenuous if they are caught in a lie. Despite any level of composure and consistency that a leader may display even in a tough-or crisis-situation, they will come across as weak if they are found to be dishonest.

No matter what their level of skill and proficiency, functional or technical, a leader will be completely ineffective if they are caught speaking anything other than the truth. Finally, a leader's character, which is demonstrated by their level of integrity, honesty, and the respect they show their followers, will be permanently tarnished if they are labeled as a liar.

LegacyMan does not need to have a Lasso of Truth wrapped around them to know that they must always be honest and speak the truth. Two things will always happen when a leader speaks the truth: they will build their credibility and they will never get caught telling a lie. LegacyMan and LegacyWoman always tell the truth.

CHAPTER 5
Captain America
Loyal

Steve Rogers wasn't always the strong, muscular, red white and blue clad World War II superhero that we know him to be. He was a scrawny fine arts student growing up during the Great Depression of the 1930s. After he failed the entrance physical to enlist in the US Army in 1940, he volunteered for Operation Rebirth. This was a project intended to enhance US soldiers to the height of physical perfection via the inventions and discoveries of Professor Abraham Erskine. Rogers eagerly became the first test subject, and after injections and ingestion of the "Super Soldier Serum", he was transformed into the perfect specimen of human efficiency. The transformation left him with greatly enhanced musculature and reflexes, and so began the adventures of Captain America.

Like all other superheroes, Captain America has many great attributes and special skills. He has a very high level of intelligence as well as agility, strength, and speed. His reaction time is superhuman. Probably the most important special quality that Captain America possess is his endurance. The Super-Soldier formula that he had metabolized as part of the experiment, enhanced not only his bodily functions to the peak of human efficiency, but importantly it gave his body the ability to eliminate the excessive build-up of fatigue-producing poisons in his muscles. This made Captain America capable of exhibiting phenomenal endurance. Wouldn't we all like that? Imagine how great it would be if we never got tired!

Captain America has many great attributes we want to see in our leaders. After all, we want intelligent, highly efficient, fast acting, and tireless leaders. However, there is one attribute that Captain America embodies, maybe more than any other superhero, that does not come because of his performance-enhancing drugs. This distinctive trait of Captain America is likely the reason he is so well loved by the masses, and why we root for him when he's in the heat of battle. Captain America is loyal! He puts the interests of his team and those he commands above all else. He cares first and foremost about ridding the world from anything and anyone who threatens that which he holds most dear: his country. He is loyal to those he serves as a leader. Like Captain America, LegacyMan must be loyal first and foremost to those he has the privilege of leading.

According to Webster's dictionary, to be loyal means to have an unswerving allegiance. This allegiance can be to one's lawful sovereign or government, but it can also mean to be faithful to a private person to whom faithfulness is due. The last two words in the previous sentence are very important to understanding loyalty. It says that loyalty is given to whom it "is due". That means, it must be earned. This leads to the obvious question of course: How do you earn loyalty? Perhaps a better question is: how do you inspire loyalty? Because loyalty is an emotion. We are loyal to that which we hold dear. Loyalty causes each of us to act in ways – even irrational ways at times – towards achieving that which is defined by the person we are loyal too. That is the fundamental power of loyalty. The leader that inspires loyalty in his or her followers, will have an army of invincible soldiers that they can mobilize towards achieving their purpose.

The first thing a leader must achieve if they want to inspire loyalty, is to get followers to be emotionally committed to them and to the vision. If we are going to be emotionally committed as followers, we need to feel first that the leader is loyal to us. We must feel like the leader cares deeply about our well-being and what is best for us. We need to be nurtured and developed by the leader. We want to be acknowledged, respected and valued by our leaders. We especially need to trust our leaders if we are going to commit our loyalty to them. Thus, they need to earn and keep our trust through their daily actions. In fact, trust and credibility are the cornerstones of loyalty. Inspiring loyalty therefore, requires an emotionally intelligent leader, connected with his followers in ways that transcends the physical, and touches the hearts and minds of their followers. It requires leaders to behave in specific ways that help people discover a greater purpose in having a relationship with them.

There are many examples we can list of how leaders-and even companies-inspired loyalty with their followers or their customers. I worked for one of the most respected companies in the world, Johnson & Johnson, for nearly eighteen years. I love J&J. It's a fabulous company that has earned its reputation over more than 100 years of acting according to a CREDO that guides ethical behavior by all its employees and leaders. The most well-known example of this was the issue that J&J dealt with back in 1982. J&J withdrew Tylenol from the marketplace after there had been an incident of seven reported deaths in Chicago, where a few people had taken extra-strength Tylenol capsules. It was reported that someone had put deadly cyanide into Tylenol capsules. It was discovered that the tampering had occurred once the product had already reached the shelves in stores. At the time, Tylenol had a commanding market share lead of more than 35% with revenues in the millions of dollars.

What did J&J do? James Burke, J&J's CEO at that time, formed a team to deal with the crisis. The guidance from Mr. Burke was simple: first, protect people and second, determine how if at all, they could save the product and the brand. Next, the company made a public announcement warning people about the consumption of the product, and they conducted an immediate product recall across the entire country of more than 31 million bottles at a cost of more than $100 million dollars. This was done despite the fact that J&J knew they were not responsible for the tampering of the product!

There is much more to the story. In fact, numerous articles and papers have been written on the subject. There are many case studies on the J&J Tylenol crisis written now used to teach business school students. It stands as an example of responsible corporate behavior. Suffice it to say that J&J acted in a highly ethical business manner, and suffered a tremendous financial loss. How was J&J rewarded for its actions? Just a few years later, Tylenol broke all sales records, and was once again – and has remained since – the number one over-the-counter pain medication chosen by consumers. In fact, it is known as the "number one trusted brand" in America. That's loyalty inspired by a leader making sure he and his team did the right thing regardless of the financial implications.

Inspiring loyalty is not easy. It takes work. It takes leaders who behave consistently according to the simple principles which we will outline below.

1. They are genuine and ethical.

The real thing: that is what the word genuine means. Genuine is the opposite of fake; and nobody likes a fake. When it comes to leadership, we all want to follow men and women that we perceive as real, honest, and people of integrity. Perhaps more important than what they say, or even how they say it, we want to follow people who are authentic. That is, we want to follow leaders who consistently say what they mean and do what they say. We especially need to follow leaders who act similarly, whether they are in a public forum or in a private setting.

The simplest definition of ethical behavior that I can think of is this: doing the right thing even when no one is watching. Can you think of a quality in a leader that we need them to display – more than any other – than ethical behavior? It is the foundation of how a leader can inspire loyalty. We need to rest in the confidence that our leader is ethical, and that they understand the difference between right and wrong. We need to know that our leaders will always chose to behave with the highest moral principles.

Leaders who are genuine and ethical inspire loyalty.

2. They are transparent.

To inspire loyalty a leader must be transparent about what they believe. Followers must never be confused or uncertain of what their leaders stand for and what their values are. Therefore, a key to a leader's success is dependent on how openly they share their ideas, and the energy with which they express their thoughts. The most effective leaders are those who consistently articulate their vision and enable their followers to connect with the direction that they are trying to take the organization.

Many of the more commonly thought of leader traits are easy to perceive. However, transparency is a trait that is often overlooked and even harder to identify. Yet, being transparent is one of the most important ways that a leader can build trust and confidence with the team.

The degree to which a leader is consistently honest, candid and open with her team is the best measure of transparency. The more transparent that the leader is perceived to be, the more followers will trust them. Moreover, there are several important benefits that a team or organization enjoy when they have a transparent leader at the helm. Among them are:

Strong, collaborative team relationships

When the leader is transparent, people are emboldened to create greater bonds with each other and with the leader. In fact, friendships are forged between team members. These strong bonds make for more communicative and effective teams. Importantly, when the leader is transparent, he or she is perceived as approachable, inclusive, and an integral part of the team, rather than just a far removed idealistic leader with no skin-in-the-game.

Speed to resolution

When teams are working well together, they can move through team dynamic stages (norming, storming, forming and performing) much more quickly. When the leader is transparent, the culture of open communications spreads across all levels of the organization and people are free – even encouraged – to share their ideas and concerns openly. There can be no doubt that a team that is communicating with no concern for office politics or fear of retribution, or any other typical road block to good communications, is going to be faster in reaching decisions and making progress towards their objectives.

Accountability

Perhaps one of the best organizational benefits enjoyed by teams led by transparent leaders is that accountability by all members of the team, soars. Under a transparent leader, people work harder and are more productive. They can feel much more empowered to take control of their own areas of responsibility. People working in these kinds of organizations take more pride in their work, and they feel beholden both to the leader and their team. The transparent leader enjoys the benefit of leading teams of people who are accountable and loyal!

3. They are trustworthy.

They say trust is earned; and if something is going to be earned, it must take some time and effort to gain it. Indeed, trust is something that traditionally takes a long time to earn.

We gain it by demonstrating consistency in behavior – usually, good behavior. Why that last distinction? Sometimes, people can earn a reputation for consistently doing the wrong thing. For example, a person can earn a reputation for constantly cheating at a game of golf. They can be "trusted" to cheat. Of course, that's not what we need in our leaders.

We want to follow people who can be trusted to put our interests ahead of their own. We enjoy following leaders who work hard to behave consistent with their stated values and those of the organization. We also want leaders who can be trusted to demonstrate a commitment to living according to the highest standards of appropriate behavior as defined by the larger societal norms that we hold sacred.

Over the course of the last thirty years of business experience and leading teams, I've learned that you earn trust first and foremost by giving it. There are implied risks in trusting someone. The unfortunate reality is that people are flawed, and, at some point there is a high probability that someone you trusted, let you down. Nevertheless, I believe that despite the risks of being let down, many of the people you trust will

work very hard to maintain it. Thus, leaders who want to gain trust quickly should start with trusting their teams. In fact, the leader should make it common practice to let their team members know they trust them, and then behave in ways that demonstrate that trust. Indeed, there are few behaviors that a leader can do to create an environment of empowerment in their organizations than to simply demonstrate trust of their teams. The trust that leaders first place on their followers, is usually well rewarded with their trust being placed on the leader in return. What should the leader do then? This is where they must dig deep into their superhero powers, and do everything humanly possible to demonstrate that they are worthy of that trust and never risk losing it!

4. They invest in people.

Perhaps the best way to earn someone's trust is to demonstrate a genuine concern and care for their personal well-being. For leaders, this translates to taking a deep interest in their follower's personal and professional development.

An inspirational leader is a role model. Someone who we want to emulate, and someone who we see as a person we can learn from. The best leaders are constantly looking for ways to develop their staff and to enable them to succeed in their personal and professional life. They stretch their staff members into new and developmental assignments, they provide proactive coaching when necessary, and connect their people to other resources to help them achieve success. It is the leaders who are perceived to be the best at people development that attract and retain the very best talented individuals.

To inspire loyalty, a leader must be a mentor, a coach, and a sponsor of people. The best leaders see their role as key in helping people improve their lives and achieve their personal goals. Perhaps one of the greatest measure of success of the legacy leader, is in their ability to be the ultimate rainmaker when it comes to talented people!

5. They embody servant leadership.

The concept of servant leadership is as old as time itself. There are in fact references to servant leadership attributed to Lao-Tzu who is believed to have lived in China in the years between 570 and 490 BC. Much has been written about the concept since then, but the phrase "servant leadership" was coined by Robert K. Greenleaf in The Servant as Leader, an essay that he first published in 1970. In that essay, Greenleaf wrote:

> *"The servant-leader is servant first... It begins with the natural feeling that one wants to serve, to serve first. Then conscious choice brings one to aspire to lead. That person is sharply different from one who is leader first, perhaps because of the need to assuage an unusual power drive or to acquire material possessions...The leader-first and the servant-first are two extreme types. Between them there are shadings and blends that are part of the infinite variety of human nature.*

> *The difference manifests itself in the care taken by the servant-first to make sure that other people's highest priority needs are being served. The best test, and difficult to administer, is: Do those served grow as persons? Do they, while being served, become healthier, wiser, freer, more autonomous, more likely themselves to become servants? And, what is the effect on the least privileged in society? Will they benefit or at least not be further deprived?*

A servant-leader focuses primarily on the growth and well-being of people and the communities to which they belong. While traditional leadership generally involves the accumulation and exercise of power by one at the "top of the pyramid," servant leadership is different. The servant-leader shares power, puts the needs of others first and helps people develop and perform as highly as possible."

At the core, the principles of servant leadership are simple, but it starts with the leader having the desire to serve. The leader's heart must be in it. This does not mean that the leader needs to be docile or meek. Instead, it's about seeing and meeting the needs of his or her followers, customers, and communities they serve.

There are many advantages of servant leadership. The concept is a long-term philosophy and way of doing things that has a positive influence on the culture of the organization. The way servant leader's treat their followers with respect and dignity engenders trust, and elevates people's desire to work hard towards achieving the vision and mission. It creates very engaged teammates, employees, and colleagues who forge a strong bond with the enterprise, and importantly, creates an environment where innovation can thrive. Ultimately the most significant advantage of servant leadership is that it leads to a boundless loyalty towards the leader.

One final thought on inspiring loyalty. It requires a hands-on approach. Any leader who inspires loyalty is typically well connected with followers, and even know many personal facts about many of their followers. Beyond their work history and performance appraisal, the loyalty inspiring leader knows about his or her follower's personal lives and interest. Loyalty comes to those leaders who are genuine, caring, and clearly seen as selfless people. These leaders are perceived as being fully aware that they impact people's lives in significant ways. LegacyWoman understands that her ultimate responsibility is to enable people to reach their full potential and lead a complete and fulfilling life. It's a responsibility they she takes seriously.

CHAPTER 6

Spiderman
Anticipate & Be Courageous

On September 4, 1929, the stock market crashed losing nearly twelve percent of its value in one day taking it to thirty-six percent off its high. On October 19, 1987, the DOW dropped almost twenty-three percent in one day – just shy of thirty-seven percent off its high. From September 2000 to January 2, 2001, the NASDAQ fell forty-six percent taking it seventy-nine percent off its all-time high. December 7, 1941 was the day President Roosevelt referred to as "a day that will live in infamy" as he announced the Japanese surprise attack on Pearl Harbor. On August 29, 2005, Hurricane Katrina devastated seventy percent of New Orleans. And on October 28, 2004, the Boston Red Sox did something they had not done since 1918: they won a World Series Championship. Imagine what you could have done differently if you had forecasted these events before they occurred. Wouldn't it be fantastic if we could accurately predict the events of the future? Making perfect decisions would be passé; after all, if you had knowledge of what was about to transpire, you could take-action to capitalize on that information. Spiderman has that ability; we call it his "spidey-sense".

Spidey-sense is Spiderman's psychic ability to know when something is about to happen, and react accordingly to prevent harm. He uses it quite effectively to protect himself and others. With his spider-sense he knows when it's time to leap from one wall to another, or when he should create a web shield to protect against some incoming firepower. Having spider-sense is akin to having your own personal radar unit. Like the systems used today to predict hurricanes and tornados, these early warning detection systems, help us to see danger before it affects us, thus allowing us to take appropriate action to abate the damage.

LegacyWoman needs to have spider-sense! She needs her own brand of early warning detection system that will allow her to properly predict and defeat things that may affect her team and organization. Spider-sense is much more than hindsight. Hindsight is simply the ability to look back and understand events that have transpired and how we could have reacted to them differently to achieve a different outcome. We can all do that! What LegacyMan needs to do is to look forward, consider what may happen next, and make decisions to ensure the best possible outcome for his organization. The leaders who can do that stand the best chance of long-term success.

Practically speaking, having "spider-sense" means having an uncanny ability to: predict immediate future conditions, quickly process the information, make the correct decision, and execute a plan of action. Of course, the last step is the most important one; after all, what use is having "spider-sense" if we don't act to capitalize on it?

Predict immediate future conditions

Spiderman's spider-sense alerts him to situations that are just about to happen moments before they do. He's not clairvoyant, knowing what's going to happen tomorrow or even an hour from now. He's not communicating telepathically with the bad guy, reading his thoughts and knowing what he's going to do before he does it. Spiderman's ability is limited to sensing the "here and now". He gets that hair-raising moment just before something bad happens, and he can react to it. That's the ability LegacyMan needs to have as well.

Spider-sense is not a superhero exclusive trait. With practice, many can develop a "sixth-sense" and effectively predict what might happen next. To develop a strong "spider-sense", LegacyMan stays in-tune with current events. A leader should remain connected to his or her organization at all levels. They keep their finger on the pulse of what's happening. Leaders should know what is on the minds of their followers, what teams are dealing with, what the customers are saying, and what the external trends and business factors are that are affecting the industry they compete in. Without the understanding that they gain from staying connected, Leaders will not develop a keen spider-sense.

Process information quickly

One of the most important skills a leader can have is their ability to process large amounts of information quickly. In today's complex global competitive environment, the factors affecting a company or a team are many. Depending on the business, a leader may be faced with understanding and considering research and development issues, regulatory issues, medical affairs issues, and manufacturing and other operational considerations. They may need to have a clear sense of global marketing strategies, distribution channels, raw material suppliers, and IT related infrastructure issues that impact their business. All of this in addition to, of course, managing the profit and loss balance sheet and protecting their shareholder's value. Leaders must be concerned with the organizational culture and infrastructure issues, personnel development, hiring and firing, and other day-to-day business demands. The leader does indeed need to be able to acquire and process a great deal of information quickly!

Importantly, what the leader must have the ability to do is distill the information that they receive into what is most relevant and important. Not one human being, not even LegacyWoman, can absorb all the information that is thrown at them. However, the most effective leaders become very good at discerning what information they need most. They understand what the leading indicators are that they must pay close attention to in their business, and they learn what questions to ask to draw out precisely what they need. Observe the most skilled leaders carefully and you will see that they each have a clear idea of what they believe are the most important indicators in their line of work, and they have determined an effective way to measure these. They have also developed a mechanism, most suited to their own personal style, on how to collect the information (i.e. what questions they ask) they need to make informed and effective decisions.

Make the correct decision

Spiderman uses his spider-sense to quickly make decisions on what he should do immediately to avoid the impending danger. What he must do, however, is not just decide, but he must make the right decision! If he chooses the wrong course of action he might create more trouble for himself. Making decisions is easy. Making the right decisions, however, is not always as simple. In a perfect world, we would have plenty of time to analyze all the factors before drawing conclusions and deciding as to what course of action we should take. However, we don't live in a perfect world, and sometimes leaders must make quick decisions. We risk not making the correct decision every time. Nevertheless, we must make decisions, and speed is often a factor.

When it comes to making decisions, leaders have a few options:

1. List advantages and disadvantages for each of the options. This approach was first suggested by Plato and popularized by Benjamin Franklin.
2. Flip a coin. Not very scientific, but it sure is quick!
3. Choose the option that seems likely to lead to the desired outcome.
4. Resort to some sort of divination technique – not recommended for LegacyMan.
5. Ask an expert what course of action should be taken.
6. Use some sort of weighted or probability scientific methodology for selecting the best solution.

7. Use intuition or "gut feeling" to decide on the best course of action.

With seven alternatives, it begs the question: which one is best for LegacyMan or LegacyWoman to use? The obvious answer is: it depends! What approach the leader takes will be a factor of the significance of the decision and the level of impact on the organization. What is most important is that the leader make a quick assessment of the situation, and then decide. That decision may be that he or she needs more data before making a final decision (as in option number 6) or that they should consult an expert (option 5) to check on the best possible approach. All too often however, the mistake leaders make is either laboring over a decision much longer than necessary, overcomplicating the issue in search of more data, or worse, they don't make the decision at all. Whatever approach the leader takes to make decisions, it should be appropriate to the situation and as timely as possible.

Execute the plan

Results don't come from a decision-making process; they come from action taken on decisions made. Planning is easy. Making decisions is also easy. Where the "rubber meets the road" is when actions are taken; until then a plan is just that – a plan. There is no risk taken when deciding what to do. There is no pain or gain in the process of deciding. It is only when decisions are converted to action that the potential to achieve anything materializes. It is also then that the potential for failure becomes real. LegacyMan is good at making decisions, but he is even better at executing them and acting to move the team, and the process, forward.

Too many leaders are lacking in this area. They talk a good game but when it comes to pulling the trigger, they fall short. There is something appealing to followers when leaders display the courage to be decisive and leaders of action. A leader needs to demonstrate commitment, and one way to do that is to be an action driven leader.

CHAPTER 7

The Green Lantern
Will Power

O ver time there have been thousands of Green Lanterns. In fact, Green Lanterns are members of the Guardians of the Universe; an intergalactic self-appointed police force known as the Green Lantern Corps. They divide the universe into 3,600 sectors, each patrolled by a Green Lantern equipped with a power ring to assist them in their duties. Interestingly, each Green Lantern is unique in their own way; but it's the special ring that gives each of the Green Lantern his power. The ring allows the user to have control over the physical world, if they have sufficient willpower and strength to use it.

In the universe of superheroes, the Green Lantern's ring has been referred to as "the most powerful weapon in the universe". Across the years, the ring has been shown capable of accomplishing anything within the imagination of the ring bearer. With the use of the ring, the Green Lantern can fly at speeds beyond that of light, travel instantaneously across the galaxy through wormholes, create protective force fields around themselves, and shoot plasma bolts to defend against opponents. The rings can even act as a computer accessing all the information needed by the super-cop. It has a universal translator to help him communicate across species, and it can help the Green Lantern travel across time – although one solitary power ring cannot generate enough power for time travel – after all we are talking about time travel! Several power rings are needed to complete this feat. These are just a few examples of what the Green Lantern can accomplish with his ring. The bottom line is that "the ring" is one impressive piece of jewelry!

The power of the ring is only limited by the wearer's will power. The greater the Green Lantern's will power, the more effective the ring will be. No two rings are exactly alike for the Green Lanterns. As it turns out, the design of each of the rings very much depends on the character and mindset of the person wearing it. One of the better known Green Lanterns, Hal Jordan, created solid, workman-like constructs for his rings. Another well-known Green Lantern, John Stewart, an architect by education had a more carefully-designed ring resembling a three-dimensional blueprint. Kyle Rayner who was an artist, has a detailed wire frame construct for his rings.

Another feature of the ring is that it generates the Green Lantern's uniform. The uniform appears and vanishes over the Green Lantern's normal attire anytime the user wills-it. With the exception that the uniform must display the symbol of the corps, the uniform varies from one Lantern to the next based on their personal preference and the social standards of their race. One important feature and power of the ring is this: when a Green Lantern is slain, their ring will automatically seek out a suitable replacement.

LegacyMan needs to have his own "power ring". He needs to have the power to move at the speed of light. Moving slow is not an option for LegacyMan. The pace he sets will be the pace that his followers will move at, and in today's global competitive environment, speed is essential. Similar to the Green Lantern, LegacyMan needs to be able to travel across galaxies – well perhaps just the globe – to unite organizations that are usually separated by geographical divides. LegacyMan needs to have the power to create protective force fields around his organization to defend against competitors and evil forces that would look to undermine his organization's objectives. He needs to have a ring that allows him access to information so that he can make sound decisions. He most certainly needs a ring with a universal translator that will allow him to effectively communicate with all members of his team. Finally, LegacyMan must always work on developing the next generation of leaders around them; in essence creating a cohort of leaders that can rise up to replace them.

However, the two most important lessons that LegacyMan must learn from the Green Lantern are these: First, it's a team effort. In the world of superheroes there is not one Green Lantern, there are many; all of them with powerful rings. When they work together they can defeat any adversary. He must go about the business of creating a team of legacymen and legacywomen, empowering them with rings of their own and aligning them to work together to achieve mutually accepted objectives. Second, they must remember that the power of their "ring" is limited only by their imaginations and will power. LegacyMan must have an abundant supply of both, imagination and will power, if they want to create the energy in their organizations that will drive extraordinary results.

Even the Lantern's powerful rings have some limitations. For instance, power rings typically require recharging every 24 hours. Although rings typically reserve a portion of their power for passive force field that protects the lantern from mortal harm. The ring also has limited effectiveness against yellow objects. By far, the most significant limitation of the power ring is the willpower of the wielder. Only pure form of willpower can make the ring effective. Finally, the ring must be intended for good use only, or the power of the ring is diminished. For example, when Superhero Green Arrow tried to use Hal Jordan's power ring against alien supervillain Sinestro, it caused him great pain and difficulty because Green Arrow's will was "cynical".

LegacyMan must learn from the limitations of the Lantern's power ring. They have to keep in mind that recharging batteries is not only a good idea, but a necessary step to ensuring their long term health and the health of the organizations they lead. The most important lesson LegacyMan must take away from the Lantern's power ring is this: attitude and intent counts! Like the Lantern's ring, LegacyMan will only be most effective when they have a positive attitude, and their intentions are pure and aimed at creating a better world around them-selves.

CHAPTER 8

Iron Man & Batman
Innovative & Breakthrough
Thinkers

*M*ore than any other Superhero, Iron Man and Batman are role models for what breakthrough thinking and innovation are all about. Perhaps the best evidence of this is the fact that Anthony Edward "Tony" Stark (a.k.a. IronMan) used his intellect, and his strong sense of preservation to invent his way out of dying! He certainly lends credence to the saying that "necessity is the mother of invention".

The story begins with Tony Stark being kidnapped while he was demonstrating experimental technologies manufactured by his company to enemies of the United States. During the kidnapping, he suffered a life-threatening heart injury. His captors keep him alive to force him to build a destructive weapon intended to be used for their evil purposes. With the help of his fellow prisoner, Nobel Prize winning physicist Ho Yinsen, they work to create a magnetic chest plate that kept the shrapnel from reaching Stark's heart, thereby saving his life.

Instead of building the weapons demanded by his captors, Stark and his new friend ingeniously created a powered armor suit that helped him escape. Thus, was born Iron Man, and Stark's new mission to help protect the world from evil people such as the ones who had kidnapped him. It is then that Stark sets about using his multinational corporation, and the resources available to him, to develop the technology and the devices that enabled him to become a superhero crime-fighter.

The character of Tony Stark is portrayed as a very intelligent and educated man. He graduated Massachusetts Institute of Technology with an electrical engineering degree by the age of 15. The boy genius received his advanced degrees in physics and engineering at the age of 21. No doubt his intellect and education were key to his success both as a business man and as Iron Man. Stark's pursuit of innovation and his breakthrough thinking mindset led him to develop all sorts of technologies. Many of these technologies and gadgets made their way into his armored suit. The uni-beam projector in its chest, pulse bolts that pick up on kinetic energy to facilitate long distance travel, an electromagnetic pulse generator, and a defensive energy shield that can be extended up to 360 degrees, are a few of the high-tech gadgets that the eccentric inventor created. Thomas Edison had nothing on Tony Stark!

Another breakthrough-thinker is the "Caped Crusader", Batman. He first appeared on the scene in 1939 as the "Dark Knight" whose secret identity is Bruce Wayne, a wealthy American playboy, philanthropist, and owner of Wayne Enterprises. As a young child, Wayne was traumatized when he witnessed his parents being brutally murdered during a robbery. He swore then to avenge his parents, and thus began his life as a crime-fighter. Like Tony Stark, Bruce Wayne possesses a high intellect, and uses his vast resources to create the most innovative gadgets to help him wage his war on crime. Also like Ironman, Batman is a superhero with no real superpowers. They both rely on intellect and technology to achieve their purpose. When confronted with situations that would lead others to simply throw in the towel, they are motivated to solve the problem. This was the case when death came knocking on Stark's door. He did not passively succumb, he used breakthrough thinking to come-up with a solution to his dilemma. For Batman, every obstacle he confronts becomes the impetus for new inventions and creative solutions. That's what makes him unique. It is these qualities of Ironman and Batman, that LegacyMan and LegacyWoman need to learn from, and adopt to make their very own.

We can't all have a genius level intellect. However, breakthrough thinking leadership does not require a PhD in rocket science. The leader's job is to create an environment where innovation and breakthrough thinking can occur. It's the leader's attitude much more than their level of education or technical aptitude, that will drive a culture of innovation. Of course, the smartest leaders are those who surround themselves with the brightest, most talented individuals that they can find, and works diligently to motivate them to achieve extraordinary feats that will make them all look like superheroes.

In my book "Breakthrough Thinking: The Legacy Leader's Role In Driving Innovation", I outlined the fundamental principles that leaders must follow to create innovative, breakthrough thinking teams. We discussed details such as: understanding of breakthrough thinking drivers, and the stages of breakthrough thinking teams. We outlined the role that leader's play in moving teams quickly through the forming, norming, storming, and performing stages and introduced a new team stage called Perstorming™. We detailed the steps that leaders must take to harness the power of individuals, and how to unleash aligned teams to create true innovation. Finally, we described the harsh realities of innovation, and the obstacles that often stand in the way of teams achieving breakthrough results consistently.

Intellectually these breakthrough-thinking principles make sense. More importantly, practically applied, these principles get results. Thus, LegacyMan should focus his attention in fostering a culture where breakthrough and innovative thinking is the norm. There are five things that a leader can do to achieve that culture:

Demand a culture of innovation

It is the leader that must set the standard and expectation that there will be an innovation culture in his or her organization. If the leader does not state it, it will not happen. Of course, simply saying it is not sufficient to make it a reality. However, as we have already learned, it's the leader's vision and his or her ability to articulate that vision clearly that will set the wheels in motion for the organization to achieve it. Thus, creating an innovation culture must be a part of that vision, and the leader must articulate clearly – and often – their desire to have an environment where the innovation is the organization's modus operandi.

Speak the language of innovation

This is the "talk-the-talk" part of the leader's job. There are few weapons in LegacyMan's armamentarium that are more powerful than his words. The leader sets the tone. What they say, and how they say it will ultimately determine the culture the organization will develop. If the leader wants to create an innovation culture, they must speak the language of innovation. That includes creating an environment where it is not only okay to challenge the status-quo, but it's the expectation to do so.

Some years ago, Hewlett Packard launched a series of television commercials where they positioned themselves as the innovation leaders in electronics. In the commercials, their people were always heard asking the question "what if?" In my estimation, that is a great leading question to generate healthy dialogue considering alternative solutions to problems – therein lies the seeds of innovation. So, ask "what if" questions often.

Invest in innovation

This is the "walk-the-talk" or the "put your money where your mouth is" part of the leader's job in creating a breakthrough thinking culture. Innovation is not free, and often it's not cheap. True innovation requires bringing the best resources available, providing them the necessary tools and equipment, and being willing to accept a higher-than-average level of risk. Driving an innovation culture is not for the faint of heart, that's why it takes a superhero like LegacyMan and LegacyWoman to make it happen.

Choke-out bureaucracy

There are few things that can kill innovation faster than procedures and bureaucracy. As the leader, no one is in a better position to challenge the processes, and to stamp-out bureaucracy wherever possible.

There are two important factors that a leader must consider if they are to be successful in eliminating bureaucratic processes from their organizations: first, they must secure support of all senior leaders and managers in their organization. It is often with these individuals that we find the strongest resistance when it comes to policies and procedures. All leaders and managers in the organization must be aligned to the idea of creating an innovation culture, and they must understand their role in making it happen. They must be held accountable to behaving in ways consistent to creating the breakthrough thinking environment. Second, the leader must be ready to re-think and change not just processes, but organizational structures as well. This will allow for experimentation and risk-taking to occur more freely throughout the organization.

Recognize innovation

Innovation is not just about creating a new teleportation system or a sophisticated holographic imaging system. Innovation can also be found in how raw materials are ordered for the manufacturing department; or in how waste materials are recovered and re-processed to minimize the environmental impact to the community. Innovation must be a part of everyone's thinking in the company, not just the folks in R&D. For that to be the case, leaders need to recognize innovation in all its forms. They also need to recognize failure when it occurs, especially when that failure come despite what might have been an innovative thought process. Learning from failure can be a great spark for the next level of innovation.

Eliminate obstacles

This is where LegacyMan's superhero strength can be essential. It's the leader's job to make sure that innovative, breakthrough thinking teams have barriers and obstacles removed from their path. These barriers can take-on many forms, and leaders need to be alert to anything that can get in the way of progress.

However, experience tells us that there are a few obstacles that seem to be the most common and show their ugly head often:

Leadership Support

Without leadership support, breakthrough thinking innovation will not take place. Without leaders at all levels adopting and working towards creating a culture of innovation, there is simply no way that it can become pervasive in the organization. Leaders must take ownership of creating the right environment, they must be committed to it, and they must all be aligned to the team's objectives. It's LegacyWoman's job to ensure that all leaders in the organization are on-board!

Organizational Politics

What's wrong with organizational politics? Check-out this definition of the term taken from BusinessDictionary.com:

"Pursuit of individual agendas and self-interest in an organization without regard to their effect on the organization's efforts to achieve its goals."

Individual agendas? Self-Interest? Without regard to the organization's effort to achieve its goals? Can any of these be good to help create an innovative, breakthrough thinking environment? Clearly, the answer is no. Thus, putting it in superhero terms, organizational politics is one of LegacyMan's arch-enemies, and it is bent on destroying all that LegacyMan is working for.

Fortunately, LegacyMan has effective weapons against organizational politics. As the source of power and influence, leaders are also the source of politics in an organization. They can smother a political climate that is negatively impacting people's attitudes, and the organization's outcomes, by aligning individual needs with organizational goals. This ensures that collective goals and individual needs are simultaneously fulfilled.

Great leaders know that organizational politics are a function of trust within the team. They also understand that trust is built on values of fairness and transparency. Hence, LegacyMan works hard to ensure that there is an overwhelming sense of fair play and transparency in communications, procedures and processes. This goes a long way in creating an environment where organizational politics take back-seat and innovation-along with a breakthrough thinking culture-take over and allow people to feel that their personal interest are satisfied along with the organization's objectives. Leaders have the ability and responsibility to ensure the team's political climate maximizes results and the satisfaction levels of the individual members of the team.

No Accountability

The word "accountability" seems to immediately connote something bad in corporate America. When we hear questions such as: "who's accountable?" or "how do we hold people accountable for performance?" our antenna shoots straight up, and we worry that something has gone wrong or is expected to go wrong. Why is that? Perhaps it's because we only look to hold people accountable when things have not gone quite the way we hoped. Accountability comes with risks; maybe that's why some people fear it.

Accountability is synonymous with responsibility, liability, answerability, and other terms that we associate with an expectation of accounting for something. When it comes to leadership, accountability is the assumption of responsibility for decisions, actions, and policies that govern the organization. It includes responsibility for everything from product quality to organizational values and individual behavior norms. All leaders are accountable. No excuses. No loopholes.

Sacred Cows

A "sacred cow" is simply an individual, organization, project, or anything else that is considered exempt from criticism or questioning. Almost every organization has its sacred cows. It might be the company president's pet project. Perhaps it's the Vice President of Marketing's son who works in the company, but really isn't doing a good job, yet no one is willing to make the tough decision of letting him go. Maybe it's the annual executive "retreat" that is supposed to be a time when company leaders do business planning, but instead everyone knows it's a boondoggle, and an excuse to play golf. It might be that R&D project that has been going on for three years, and seems to be draining resources while getting nowhere fast, but no one seems willing to kill the project. Whatever it is, sacred cows are real, they are innovation killers, and they are resource hogs. If LegacyWoman is going to create a truly innovative and breakthrough thinking environment, she must make sure that sacred cows end-up on the butcher's block.

Risk Aversion & Fear

To create innovation, you must take risks. With those risks come the fear of failure and the consequences of that failure. When it comes to taking risk LegacyMan has only a few rules: take prudent, but aggressive risk, reward risk takers, and learn from the risks that lead to failure. Only the leader can minimize the effect of fear in an organization and encourage risk taking. They must consistently model the behavior themselves, and they must make certain that when failure occurs, it is dealt with appropriately. People will watch with keen interest to see how the first pioneer risks takers who fail, are dealt with. Wouldn't you do the same thing? Leaders who want to create a fearless environment need only treat risk takers fairly and transparently; learning from their failures and rewarding them handsomely for success!

Analysis Paralysis

One indicator of the level of risk tolerance that an organization or a team has, is how much analysis goes into every decision made. The amount of data gathering and analysis that goes into a decision is directly proportional to the impact of the decision. However, not all decisions are created equal. If a facilities team is trying to determine what the best color scheme is to use when renovating the company training room, it might seem foolish and a waste of resources to do a survey of 500 employees to get their opinion before moving forward. Would it surprise you to know that this happened in a company I worked at? The impact of that decision simply did not deserve such a high level of analysis. A better approach would have been to pick a color, go with it, and in the unlikely event that it ended-up making people sick to look at it, then paint it again a different color. The cost of doing that would have been much less than the cost of the time and effort it took to survey 500 people and analyze the survey results before deciding. Here's the ironic part of the story: in the end, the color they chose was exactly the one they had initially considered.

On the other hand, if a medical team is trying to determine what the best approach would be to conduct a heart transplant procedure on a patient, it would seem reasonable that they would want to have all the data at their disposal that could influence their decisions and the ultimate outcome of the procedure. A robust methodical collection of the data, running tests, and analyzing the results seem quite appropriate in a situation where life and death are involved.

Leaders must help create an environment where teams are empowered to make decisions with appropriate levels of data. This means that sometimes decisions will be made with imperfect or incomplete information, and that the inherent risks associated with those decisions are understood and accepted. Don't allow teams to spin their wheels in eternal analysis paralysis mode!

Lack of Focus or Shifting Priorities

Innovative and breakthrough thinking teams are flexible. They can make quick course corrections to accommodate changing environmental and business demographics, initiate new projects to capitalize on emerging opportunities, and even do a good job of cutting-off projects when it's clear that they are not yielding the expected results.

Another way that innovation can be stifled in an organization is if there is a lack of laser-like focus or shifting priorities. It is important that leaders don't allow their teams to fall prey to "the flavor of the month" club. That is when priorities – and the associated projects – seem to go through a revolving door, coming and going, according to some whim or undefined objective. LegacyMan understands the need to have a clear and definitive vision and objectives to help focus the team and drive organizational results. Change is not a bad thing. Change that is not linked or understood as part of the overriding strategy to achieve the stated objectives however, can be. When this kind of change becomes prevalent it generates an attitude of "wait and see". People sit back and wait to see what will happen next. They might ask themselves: why work on a project or initiative only to have it change or be eliminated when the next initiative comes into vogue? Thus, the leader works to ensure that there is good balance between changing direction to capitalize on new opportunities or make appropriate course corrections, and simply having an ineffective culture of "shifting priorities."

Regardless of industry, business segment, or region of the world that they operate in, winning teams have a culture of innovation and breakthrough thinking in common. It's up to the leader to set the pace and to do all that is necessary to foster the environment where creativity and risk taking – both critical elements of innovation – can flourish and establish deep roots in the organizational DNA.

CHAPTER 9

The Hulk
Emotionally Intelligent

"Hulk smash!" This is about 50% of The Hulk's total spoken vocabulary. He simply is a "man" of few words; he is more the action type. The Hulk can go almost anywhere he wants. He is however, the quintessential "bull in a china shop". Wherever he goes, he leaves a wreck behind with smashed cars, buildings, roads, and especially, bad guys. Nevertheless, he is considered one of the most beloved superheroes. There is something we all love about this green giant.

The first appearance of this fictional character came in 1962 when he was created by Stan Lee and Jack Kirby. In his comic book appearances, the Hulk is a green-skinned and muscular humanoid, possessing a vast degree of physical strength. When he is not the hulk, he's none other than the mild-manored,

Dr. Bruce Banner. Dr. Banner, is a brilliant physicist, socially awkward, emotionally reserved, and physically weak. In other words, nothing like his alter ego, the Hulk.

How does a gentle scientist become a ferocious, almost uncontrollable beast? In the case of Dr. Banner, it all started when he was accidentally exposed to gamma radiation during the detonation of an experimental bomb. The effects of the radiation transformed Banner into the Hulk when he is subjected to emotional stress. Whether he gets angry on his own or against his will, he undergoes a metamorphosis that leads him to physically change from a scrawny nerdy scientist, to the destructive muscle-bound beast.

Throughout his exploits, once he discovers the beast within, Dr. Banner does everything possible to avoid getting angry. He knows that if he does become angry, he will lose control, become something he does not want to be, and inevitably, cause damage to people and things around him that he may later regret. Bruce Banner has learned the lessons of having a high degree of "emotional intelligence" the hard way! LegacyWoman and LegacyMan can take this lesson from the

Hulk. They must have a high degree of emotional intelligence and learn to control the beast within.

All leaders get angry. We are all human and subject to the same range of emotions. The best leaders are not those that don't get angry. In fact, the best leaders channel their emotions, learn to manage them, and in some cases, are even able to use them to move their agenda forward. Showing emotion is not necessarily a bad thing. However, letting those emotions control us, and cause us to act in destructive and harmful ways, is damaging. This is easier said than done, but it is critically important for the effectiveness of the leader, and their long-term credibility, that they learn to manage their emotional barometer.

In their book, "The 15 Commitments of Conscious Leadership", Jim Dethmer, Diana Chapman and Kaley Klemp, offer three creative tips on how to effectively use anger. Below is an excerpt from their book:

"1. Feel Your Anger, Don't Repress It

Many leaders were taught to repress their anger. Great leaders know this doesn't work. When you repress your anger two things can happen. First, you'll probably get sick. Research suggests unfelt anger make people sick. Common anger-related illnesses include chronic back pain, heart disease, high blood pressure, headaches, TMJ and depression. Second, you can waste energy. Repressing anger is like holding a beach ball under water. It takes lots of energy. Great leaders value energy, they don't waste it.

2. Express Your Anger, Don't Hide It

Many leaders are taught not to express their anger. This is a bad idea and odds are you won't fool anybody. The human species operates like pack animals. We've learned to sense how others in the pack, especially leaders, are feeling. It is key to our survival. When you're angry, people around you know it no matter how hard you try to hide it. They'll react by fleeing, fighting or freezing. This behavior wastes time and energy.

Great leaders learn to express anger. They do this in healthy, direct, non-aggressive and non-toxic ways. Great leaders simply and powerfully say, "I feel angry." They don't say, "I'm angry at you because you dropped the ball." Or, "I'm angry because we missed our quarterly earnings." All explanation and justification are a waste of time.

3. *Learn From Your Anger, Don't Waste It*

Average leaders waste their anger by getting embroiled in drama-based debates fueled by blame. They get stuck wanting to prove they're right. Great leaders know this is a massive waste of time and energy. Though it might be fun for the ego to parade around its smarts, nothing of value is accomplished. Instead of blaming others, great leaders learn from anger and become even better leaders."

These authors have really captured the essence of how a leader should deal with their anger very succinctly and elegantly. Is this an easy thing to learn to do? No, it's not. Just like all worthwhile skills, learning to manage our anger and use it effectively takes practice and persistence. The rewards are significant for the leader and the organizations they lead.

Anger: A powerful emotion

Anger is a very powerful emotion. If you are too angry, or angry often, people tend to fear or try to avoid you. If you keep it bottled up, you become like a tea-pot about to boil over or a pressure cooker about to blow its top. Either extreme is not good. Having a healthy level of Emotional Intelligence (EQ) is the key to balance when it comes to dealing with anger. EQ is the capability of individuals to recognize their own and other people's emotions, distinguish between different feelings, and label them appropriately. The concept of EQ has been around since the early 1960s, but it really came into vogue in 1995 when Daniel Goleman wrote his book "Emotional Intelligence".

The ideas behind EQ are captured in three main models: the ability model, the trait model, and the mixed model. It is not this author's intention to diminish the incredible amount of research and work that has been done by many to put forth these models, nor will I try to expand on them in this short text. However, for our purposes, and to the topic of dealing with anger, the mixed model introduced by Goleman is the most appropriate to expand on our discussion.

This model focuses on an array of competencies and skills that drive leadership performance. Goleman's model outlines five important areas that he believes help better describe a leader's effectiveness. He described them in his 1998 article "What Makes a Leader" as:

- Self-awareness: the ability to know one's emotions, strengths, weaknesses, drives, values and goals and recognize their impact on others while using gut feelings to guide decisions.

- Self-regulation: involves controlling or redirecting one's disruptive emotions and impulses, and adapting to changing circumstances.

- Social skill: managing relationships to move people in the desired direction.

- Empathy: considering other people's feelings especially when making decisions.

- Motivation: being driven to achieve for the sake of achievement.

Considering these five areas carefully, it becomes evident that having the ability to recognize and understand emotions - especially our own - and then use that information to guide our decision-making process, will be helpful in managing anger effectively. Staying aware of the situation around us, and how we are feeling at that moment, will better enable us to manage each situation appropriately. This is especially important for leaders who must ensure they are always in-tune with how their actions will affect the people around them.

Controlling the Beast

What are some steps we can proactively take to better manage our anger, and make sure it does not get the best of us?

Avoid getting angry in the first place

First, and it may seem like an obvious thing to say, but try avoiding getting angry as much as possible. If you think about it, the number of things worth getting angry about, are few. A smart leader is very selective about what they allow themselves to get angry over. That does not mean we should suppress our feelings, but rather we become more selective over what we allow to turn us into the Hulk.

Temper your response

Secondly, make every effort to control the temperature of your response to a situation. Making sure that our response is appropriate and proportional to the stimulus causing the anger is a sign of a mature and emotionally intelligent leader. It takes quite a bit of stimulation to get Dr. Banner to turn into the Hulk. He tries everything he can to avoid letting the green monster out of its cage. It is best if we vent our anger in-line with the situation.

Don't get angry over things you can't control

Third, don't get angry over things you can't control. In addition to being futile, getting angry over things we can't control adds a special level of stress to our teams and those we lead. If they perceive that the leader is angry or reacting negatively to something beyond their control, it leads to frustration and lack of credibility for the leader. For instance, if the economy takes a turn for the worst, and the local currency in a country, say like Russia, devalues by 50% in a matter of one year, essentially wiping-out the profit of the sales in that country overnight for your company, getting upset over this will lead nowhere. If this sounds like a very specific example rooted in personal experience, it is! Just a few years ago, that is precisely what happened to my business. Currencies in many countries, like Russia, Korea, and even European countries, became weaker against the US dollar. For many USA based companies, this meant that overnight, their profits dropped significantly year-over-year. No doubt this was very frustrating for all of us. However, to get angry over it, would have sent the wrong signal. Instead, we channeled that emotion to figure out how to best overcome the challenges to our business.

Do this when anger strikes

Donald Gibson of Fairfield University, who co-wrote "Managing Anger in the Workplace" offers the following strategies for controlling anger when it strikes:

- *Take several deep breaths*
- *Repeat a calming word or phrase in your mind such as "relax" or "stay calm"*
- *Slowly count to 10*
- *Ask yourself: "how would my favorite leader handle this situation?"*

- *Avoid tensing your muscles. As soon as you can, close your eyes and consciously think to unclench your jaw and loosen your muscles*
- *Listen to your favorite music*
- *When you are feeling angry after you leave work, change clothes as soon as you get home. This simple gesture will help you change your state of mind*

At first glance, these may seem rather simple. Perhaps to the typical "type red" leader personality, these techniques may even feel rather foolish to put into action. However, these are all great coping mechanisms, and-take it from someone with experience-they work. No doubt we can each come up with a few others that would help us lower our own temperature, and regain our senses when we get angry. For me, one of the most effective things that I can do to avoid having the wrong reaction when I am angry, is to hit the "pause" button. If possible, simply putting the conversation on hold, is a good way to regain composure, and re-engage later when things have calmed down. That also provides us an opportunity to refocus our attention on something more productive. This can be done, even in the middle of a meeting. When a topic is getting too heated and anger starts to boil over, it can be a very effective technique to call for a pause. Perhaps even to park the topic for a few minutes or a few hours if necessary. This gives all parties the opportunity to mentally compose themselves, and come back to the conversation when minds are clear of negative emotions.

No one wants to work with, or for, the Hulk. There is too much collateral damage when the Hulk is done smashing things. Leaders must avoid allowing their temperament to get the best of them, and they must know themselves well enough to know how to remain calm, cool and collected – especially when everyone else around them is not. The bottom line on EQ and dealing with anger for LegacyMan is this: control the beast or it will control you.

CHAPTER 10

Aquaman
Adaptable

Aquaman may not be one of the more recognizable figures among today's contemporary superhero fans, but this fictional character has staying power! He is among the superheroes created back in the 1940s by Paul Norris and Mort Weisinger. According to his first origin, Arthur Curry, also-known-as, Aquaman, was the son of Atlanna, an Atlatean princess, and Tom Curry, an ordinary human and light-house keeper she fell in love with. Much like Superman, as a child, Arthur was unaware of his special origins and powers. It wasn't until later that he discovered he had the ability to breathe underwater. He also learned of his mother's true-identity, and that he had inherited the ability to communicate telepathically with, and control all, marine life. Interestingly, his power is usually most easily used to affect sea creatures, but he also has the power to affect any being that lives upon the sea, or is somehow associated with the sea.

It is Aquaman's adaptability that impresses me most, and it is that trait that Legacy Leaders, our LegacyWoman and LegacyMan, must aim to emulate. We live in an ever-changing, fast-pace, global-economy world. The most effective leaders are those who, not only embrace change and adapt to it, but those who thrive in changing environments. Indeed, the leader's adaptability – their ability to read the landscape in which their organization must play, and to lead their teams despite the changing environment - will be one of the most important traits of effective leaders going forward.

Given the importance of being adaptable as a leader, it leads to an obvious question: how does one become more adaptable? To answer that question, we should start by answering the question: what are the qualities of someone that would be considered "adaptable"? When I think of a person who is adaptable, I attribute to them the following traits:

1. They are open-minded.
2. They listen well and consider other view-points.

3. They carefully evaluate current conditions and anticipate what might happen next.

4. They are not defeated by failure, rather they are emboldened by it.

5. They don't panic in unexpected situations.

6. They do not remain stubborn in their positions and are willing to experiment with new ideas and approaches.

7. They are intellectually curious, and always aiming to learn something new.

More than anything, being adaptable is a mindset. It's not a mindset that comes naturally or easily to everyone. The good news is that it can be a learned behavior. It requires practice and developing "muscle memory" so that we consistently behave in ways that demonstrate that we are indeed adaptable and learning leaders. A few ways that we can practice at being adaptable are:

1. Stay-up to date with the latest business enabling technologies. This does not mean we should adapt every new gadget, but we should make sure to remain current with tools that enable us and our teams to be more effective.

2. Always ask the "why" and "why not" questions. Constantly pushing yourself, and those you lead, to

be curious and explore the answer to those simple questions. This will help keep the team thinking about new ideas to solving problems.

3. Eliminate "no" from the vocabulary. This does not mean saying yes to everything. It simply means we need to resist the temptation to start with "no". When we start from a negative position, it quickly shuts down the innovation process. Instead, we should use positive language and words that embolden our teams to try new and creative ways of working.

4. Schedule routine brainstorming sessions with your team. It's important to pull the team together, not just when there is an urgent situation that needs to be dealt with, but rather gather them when the team has time to think creatively without the urgency of a crisis. Giving the team an opportunity to flex their creative muscles for no other reason than to find new ways of doing things better and faster, can be incredibly empowering and motivating to the team.

5. Stay out of your comfort zone. The best leaders are aware of what their comfort zones are, and they proactively stay clear of them. Purposefully putting yourself in different

situations and forcing the need to adapt to change will help keep that important life-skill well-tuned. It will also help people around you develop the same skillset.

6. Remain curious. Great leaders ask great questions. Remaining inquisitive and considering options before coming to a judgement or deciding on a course of action, are also traits of the best leaders. Importantly, leaders understand that the greater the diversity of ideas, the more robust the ultimate decisions made will be. The best way to get ideas on the table is to ask for them!

Adaptability as a leadership trait is very significant. It is driven in part by the fast pace of change in all business segments – private and public – and the lightning speed of technological changes. In today's world, news travels across the planet in a mere few seconds, and nations are linked together by economic, political, and at times, social agendas. One thing that remains constant, is that change will be inevitable, and it will continue relentlessly. Leaders all over the world are facing change and complexity. Thus, the ability to adapt is not optional for leaders. Simply coping with change is not sufficient.

It's clear that the most successful leaders going forward will be those who are best at being adaptable. The inverse corollary of this statement is even more important: inflexible leaders limit the adaptability of others. If a leader is non-adaptive, he or she will limit the creativity of their teams, and will likely stifle innovation in the organization. Team moral will be jeopardized, and empowerment will be a distant memory as the team will settle into a routine where change is avoided and considered a bad thing.

Aquaman has many superhuman powers. Additional to incredible strength, he can see in near total darkness, and has enhanced hearing. Although he can remain underwater indefinitely, he grows weak if he remains on land – out of his primary element – for extended periods of time. No doubt this is a very formidable character. All of his great traits stem from his ability to adapt. It is his ability to adapt that allows him to live and thrive in the harshest of underwater environments. LegacyMan and LegacyWoman must learn from Aquaman, and work diligently to develop the skill of being a learning and adaptable leader. This is more than a survival trait for a leader. It is, in fact, a significant differentiator that will separate the average leader from the extraordinary superhero leader.

CHAPTER 11

Wolverine Regenerate

*L*ogan, also known as Wolverine, is a very popular superhero character first created in the early 1970s. His debut was in an appearance along with the Incredible Hulk before getting his own "major role" in 1974. Wolverine is a part of a superhero team referred to as X-Men. Born James Howlett, Logan first appeared in Marvel comics, as a mutant human with keen animal senses. Wolverine has enhanced strength and physical capabilities, and has very strong retractable bone claws in each hand that can inflict havoc on his opponents.

Wolverine has many formidable qualities. There can be no doubt however, that his most significant and unique trait, is his powerful ability to regenerate. Logan is a fearless warrior who takes on the fiercest opponents with incredible zeal. In the heat of battles, Wolverine takes down his opponents with great agility and strength. However, you can't be in heated battle after battle, and expect to come-away without a few bruises or – worst yet – a few profusely bleeding wounds. This is certainly true for Logan. The difference being, when he gets injured, he's only down temporarily as his body possesses the healing factor that allows him to regenerate and recover quickly, enabling him to re-engage in the battle. It is this unique ability, and his near limitless energy, that provide important lessons for LegacyWoman and LegacyMan. They too must be able to re-generate, recover, and get back in the battle after they've been injured.

All leaders face a simple reality: they are targets. By virtue of their position, the visible stances they take, and the need to be exposed to a team and the organizations they lead, they are constantly in the crosshair of potential criticism. They are especially vulnerable if they lead larger organizations, and are exposed to broader public audiences. Thus, knowing how to deal with direct, or even subtle attacks, and quickly regenerating to recover, is a critically important skill for all leaders. Let's look at a few ways that leaders can learn to cope with criticisms and use their own internal healing powers to stay in the game and remain effective.

Mental health, personal balance, and clarity

Maintaining a healthy level of mental sanity, while staying balanced in our response to stimuli is an important way to stay focused and clear. A few simple actions that leaders can take to keep themselves in check are:

- Exercise regularly: the positive effects of exercise have been well documented. Having a routine exercise regiment, will go a long way to keeping the leader clear of mind, while counteracting some of the stress levels that can derail them, and cause them to lose focus.

- Engage in hobbies and extra-curricular activities: The type of hobby is not what is important, but having interests that occupy our minds, and a some of our time, is valuable. In fact, a hobby or activities that requires more than our minds, but also engages our body, is also beneficial. Sometimes, just gardening, working on our home's landscape with our own hands, painting, doing wood-work, or engaging in some other manual task, is a terrific way to distract us from the stressful work environment. These actions can release our minds - albeit temporarily - to give us time to regenerate.

- Meditate: Few activities can have more therapeutic value than simply being still and clearing the brain. Even if we simply spend some quiet time sitting in our offices, it can help reduce stress levels and provide clarity of mind that enables us to tackle what's next.

- Laugh often and whistle while you work: They say laughter has great healing powers. I believe that is true. Even in the hardest of situations, finding something to laugh about – regardless of how brief a time that is – will keep us grounded and centered in our own minds. Much to my youngest daughter Marisa's shagreen, I enjoy whistling. I do it often, and even sometimes while I am at work. It helps me relax, and settles me down when I need it most. It's hard to be angry and whistle at the same time. When things get a bit heated, or I am dealing with a difficult situation, if the conditions permit, I go for a brief walk, and whistle a few tunes. I can attest to its medicinal effects, not just for yourself, but for those around you. So, leaders, lighten-up, laugh more, and whistle while you work!

Rely on your inner circle of friends

Every leader needs to have an intimate circle of friends and confidants that they can count on to help keep them in check when necessary. Having such a group of people provides us a place to be vulnerable, and expose our fears and concerns – yes, even LegacyMan has fears and concerns. Such a core group of individuals can also be counted on to nurture us, correct us when necessary, and allow us a place to off-load emotional baggage when needed. The best leaders are very thoughtful of who they bring into their inner circle, and rely on them heavily to guide their thinking and actions daily.

Don't take things personally and Pause before responding

One of the hardest things to do when we are under attack, is not to push back. It goes against our very instinct. Yet that is precisely what smart leaders do. In today's virtual and connected world, it is especially easy to respond to emails, text messages, and tweets with lighting speed, rather than taking the time to consider a measured response to a criticism or some other attack on us. LegacyWoman has the inner strength to fight the urge of lashing back at an attacker, and she avoids knee-jerk reactions. Rather than lowering herself to the bowel of a debate, she takes the highroad and provides a measured and elegant response that properly captures the facts of whatever the issue is. She calmly thinks about the best way to clarify her position, consistent with her vision and actions, and lays out her position in a logical and non-emotional way.

Leaders need to remember that criticism comes with the job and they don't take it personally.

Deflate the attack

One of the best ways to regenerate as a leader after being attacked is to disarm the person or group attacking us; and one of the most elegant ways of doing that is to admit mistakes. LegacyMan and LegacyWoman are not afraid to admit their mistakes. We don't expect our leaders to be infallible. We do however, expect them to be accountable for their actions, learn from their mistakes, and press-on. The leader who admits their mistakes openly and humbly, is often rewarded with increased trust and the opportunity to fix the problem.

Another way to disable an attacker or a critic is to effectively use allies to support our position, and allow them to express points of view that directly counter those being made by the opposition. However, this only works when our allies are armed with truthful facts, and can articulate these facts in ways that helps provide clarity to the issues being debated. This is very different from the "spinning of information" we often see, especially in political circles, where one attack prompts an equal or more severe attack by the other side. This is counterproductive, leads to distrust of the leader, and at a minimum reduces the leader's credibility. LegacyMan understands full well the importance of always remaining truthful and transparent to their "true north" in communications. This is the best way to disarm and dispute the criticism or attack that comes our way.

The leader's ability to maintain clear focus and regenerate mentally, is a critical skill that weighs heavily on the level of success they will achieve. Wolverine wins when he fights, not because he does not get hurt. He wins because he regenerates when he is injured, uses the natural anger and energy that comes from being attacked, and channels it back to fighting back intelligently to beat his opponent. As a leader, LegacyMan knows that he will be attacked and probably injured. The knowledge of the pain they will inevitably suffer does not deter them from taking on the battle however; much to the contrary, it emboldens them to fight on, knowing that they can regenerate. Although the leader may be down while the wounds heal, the best leaders use that time to re-group, re-set, and re-engage. The ability to regenerate is an important trait of the finest leaders.

CHAPTER 12

The Fantastic Four Flexibility, Transparency, Passion, and Durability

The Fantastic Four are a superhero team that made their appearance as a Marvel Comics phenome in 1961. These ordinary humans, are exposed to cosmic rays during a scientific mission to outer space, and upon returning to earth from their ill-fated mission, are transformed into four extraordinary individuals with impressive, albeit rather strange, abilities. They are not only unique in their skills, but in the way that they operate as a team; something that is different from other superheroes who typically work more as lone rangers.

The first of the Fantastic Four is Reed Richards, a.k.a. Mister Fantastic. He is a scientific genius and the leader of the group, who was transformed into a human rubber-band, and who can stretch his body into incredible lengths and shapes. Next, is Susan Storm, a.k.a. the Invisible Woman. Sue can make herself invisible at will, and can project powerful invisible force fields. The more rebellious and "free-spirit" member of the team is Sue's younger brother, Johnny Storm, a.k.a. the Human Torch. He can engulf himself in flames, and use the energy to fly at amazing speeds. Finally, there is Ben Grimm, a.k.a. the Thing. Ben was the good, and even gentle friend, with the grumpy disposition who becomes the monstrous stone-like flesh humanoid with superhuman strength, durability, and endurance.

The Fantastic Four have often been portrayed as a dysfunctional, yet loving, family. It's probably one of the things we like about them, and it can be entertaining to see them bickering over silly things like most families and friends do from time to time. However, what is probably most notable about the Fantastic Four, in addition to their unique individual traits and strengths, is that they commit themselves to the advancement of scientific achievement and the betterment of society at large. Despite their bickering, the Fantastic Four come together with a single mind and purpose to form an invinsible team in times of crisis. There is much that LegacyMan and LegacyWoman can learn from this team of superheroes about being flexible, transparent, passionate, and durable.

Flexibility

Flexibility is defined as the ability to adapt to change. Flexible leaders can change their plans, and they are able to match their actions to the situation. They are also great at maintaining calm during periods of great disorder and chaos. The ability to flex is a tremendously important skill for a leader to embody. Leaders that excel at flexibility embrace change, they can deal effectively with ambiguity, and are in-touch with their constituents in a way that informs their decisions.

Fortunately, flexibility is a skill that can be developed. Much like the flexibility we gain when we stretch our bodies consistently, leaders can exercise their way to becoming increasingly nimble and flexible. There are two ways for leaders to improve their flexibility:

- Practice Situational Leadership: The Situational Leadership model was developed by Ken Blanchard and Paul Hersey in the mid 1970's. My first exposure to this model was while I was an Air Force Cadet completing my officer training. I have applied the model throughout my career, and it works. Simply stated, there is no single style that leaders should apply in every situation. In fact, the most successful leaders are those that can flex their position, and adapt their style to help drive team and individual performance. There is more to this powerful model and tool for leaders to learn and adapt, and I would very much recommend all leaders take a training on Situational Leadership as it will make them much more effective.

- Be self-aware and manage personal style: Although it is probably one of the least discussed leadership competencies, self-awareness is one of the most valuable. Leaders who are aware of their style, their strengths, and their weaknesses, are more effective at connecting with their followers. They are usually less stubborn, and more open considering ideas other than their own. In his book "Heart, Smart, Guts and Luck", Anthony Tjan wrote:

"there is one quality that trumps all, evident in virtually every great entrepreneur, manager, and leader. That quality is self-awareness. The best thing leaders can do to improve their effectiveness is to become more aware of what motivates them and their decision-making."

The smart leader works hard, and consistently over time, to remain in-touch with their personal style, and how to flex it to be the most effective leader they can be. Perhaps the greatest benefit that leaders gain from being self-aware is the trust they gain from those they lead, and the increase in credibility that surely comes with that trust.

Transparency

As we outlined in Chapter 5, one of the benefits of a leader being transparent is that it inspires follower loyalty. There are other inherent benefits to a leader consistently behaving in ways that preserve their reputation as honest, direct, and consistently transparent. In organizations where the leader is transparent, speed to problem solving is improved, innovation accelerates, and team and individual relationships flourish. In organizations with transparent leaders, genuine friendships emerge among colleagues, teams move quickly through developmental stages, and trust among team members soars. Ultimately, in organizations where leaders are transparent, a culture of empowerment emerges that enables the team to achieve great results.

Indeed, the benefits of transparent leadership are clear. Achieving transparency however, can be challenging. There are specific actions and strategies that leaders can use to improve their ability to act transparently. Here are a few actions that will improve transparency:

- Communicate precisely, simply and clearly: The way we speak, and the way we express ourselves in emails, text messages, or any other form of communication is critical. Keeping the message simple, consistent, and as complete as possible is an excellent way for the leader to create a feeling of transparency and trustworthiness.
- Seek and consider feedback openly: Good leaders proactively ask for, and think about feedback. They work hard to remain approachable and open to all members of the team speaking out, regardless of their title or level in the organization. The best leaders however, are those who

wisely incorporate the feedback they get into the direction the team is taking. This drives a culture of empowerment like nothing else! When team members are heard by the leader, and they see their ideas turned into action, it emboldens them to make even greater contributions.

- Slam open the doors and encourage less behind closed-door meetings. This idea is simple: have fewer meetings that remain cloaked in secrecy; instead share information freely and openly whenever possible. These actions build trust and leader credibility.

- Make certain that the office environment supports transparency: the office layout is important and sends a clear signal as to the culture of the organization. Where possible, move to an open floor concept, with less offices, have more meetings in rooms with clear glass so that people can be seen, and create common areas where individuals can gather for impromptu brainstorming sessions. The most creative companies have this kind of environment in common.

- Make fewer decisions directly and delegate more responsibility. This idea may seem counterintuitive to some leaders, and may even be impossible for a few.

However, leaders must aim at making fewer decisions rather than more. That is precisely what the smartest leaders do. They allow their teams to make as many of the decisions as possible. If we as leaders have done a great job communicating our vision, the mission and the end-in-mind, if we have set the proper expectations for ethical behaviors, and if we have surrounded ourselves with the very best people we could recruit, then we need to leave it to them to make decisions.

- Cultivate a working environment that rewards employees who display the traits of transparent team members. A proper reward system, both formal and informal, are necessary in every organization where humans are involved. Everyone likes to be appreciated and recognized for their efforts. Good leaders understand the power of "thank you", and they are not afraid to use it.

- Make a promise; keep a promise. We expect leaders to say what they will do, and do what they have said. The leader that does this consistently is richly rewarded with all the benefits that come along with being a transparent leader.

Fiery Passion

Passion. The very word engenders a feeling like no other in the English language. It's a strong emotion that evokes even a physical reaction. Our temperature rises, our pupils get dilated, and our heartrate speeds up. When we are under the effects of passion, we can even experience the unique medical condition known as *cutis anserina* – also known as "goose bumps".

When we think of someone as passionate, we say they have a "fire in the belly". A passion is something or someone that has captured our imagination, and to which we are dedicated and committed to with unwavering resolve. For some – the lucky ones-a passion is what wakes them every morning, and it is what fills their days. It's what they think about most, and it is that "thing" that propels them to action. For leaders, having a vision is paramount. Indeed, for leaders, having a mission to guide them, is critical. However, it is passion that drives the best leaders. It is the reason for their existence. Without a fiery passion, leaders and the organizations they lead, will only reach the heights of mediocrity rather than the pinnacle of their potential success.

The fact is that people who are passionate about what they do, are successful at it. It's not the skills, knowledge or even education that are the primary drivers and predictors of success. Passion is.

Passionate people take more risks. They don't accept failure as an end-outcome. Instead, they use failure as a motivator to try harder. They don't listen to naysayers bent on derailing them, and they don't waste any time with negative people who have phrases like "it can't be done" in their vocabulary. LegacyMan and LegacyWoman are passionate people. They have an inner strength, and an unlimited supply of energy to dedicate to their vision. They recognize that their job is first and foremost to infect everyone in their organization with the same level of optimism and excitement about the mission.

Passionate leaders ignite passion in their followers, and they can produce an energy within their teams that propels breakthrough thinking. Finally, the passionate leader has a positive and contagious attitude, champions his or her people, is a cheerleader who enthusiastically rewards people and performance, and is someone who remains eternally optimistic. One more thing about a passionate LegacyMan: he's invincible.

Durability and Thick Skin

In a previous chapter, we spoke of Wolverine. We admired his "regenerative" powers whereby he can quickly heal when wounded. That is indeed an impressive power, and a very necessary one for a leader to possess. After all, as leaders, we are targets, and we are bound to be wounded at some point or another. Whether by a rival competitive attack, or because we make a mistake of our own doing, leaders are often wounded. Having the ability to heal and recover from that wound, and get back in the game is critical to a leader's success.

Perhaps a better way to "stay-in-the-game" is not to get wounded in the first place. That's what makes Ben Grimm – The Thing – so amazing. He has skin that is literally as hard as rock. Getting through that thick skin of his takes much more than the ordinary weaponry available to most of his enemies. The Thing is durable! LegacyWoman and Legacy Man must also be durable. They choose carefully that which they allow to penetrate under the hard outer-shell of their body, to get "under their skin", and make smart judgements on how to respond when it does happen.

Having a thick skin is important and it does not mean that you don't care. It means that only those things that you allow to affect you, do. Caring about something does not mean that we should let it color our judgment, and bias our thinking on an issue. Leaders that develop a thick skin are better able to maintain their perspective on whatever the issue is, and it enables them to think rationally about what an appropriate response - positive or negative - should be

There are a few ways that leaders can develop a thick skin:

- Don your "Teflon jacket". Polytetrafluoroethylene, a.k.a. Teflon, was discovered in 1938 by Dr. Roy Plunkett. This non-stick coating is used in all sorts of products. Since the 1970s, the nickname "Teflon" has had a negative connotation when used to described a leader. It's usually a criticism intended to describe a person to whom bad things don't stick whether they deserve it or not. Although this nickname isn't given as a moniker of praise, it could have a positive meaning if we think of the ability to let what critics shoot at us, slide off as if though we were wearing a Teflon vest. As we've mentioned, leaders are targets and they will face criticism. It is important that they don't dwell or spend too much mental energy on it. They need to let it go and let it "slide off" their chest.

- Stay humble. One way that we can disarm our attackers and nay-sayers, is to remain humble and willing to accept the criticism elegantly. The best leaders can absorb a punch, and resist the temptation to fight back. This is not to say that leaders should not respond to any criticisms or attacks. It simply means that they should respond from a position of strength rather than emotion. The smart leader takes the time to consider the feedback, thinks carefully about it, and takes the high-road when responding.

- Choose your battles carefully: The best response to some attacks is no response at all. The smart leader is thoughtful about the criticisms they choose to engage in, and those they wisely ignore. In today's connected environment, we can respond to emails and tweets, and other forms of communication at the speed of light. It is increasingly difficult to resist responding the moment we receive a message. That's usually a mistake, as we may be responding from an emotional state. It is always best to think about what to say and do, calmly consider our response if one is needed, and respond with a professional tone and a plan of action.

- Find the pearls of wisdom in the criticism and learn from critics. The harshest criticisms to take usually have some truth to them. In the middle of an attack, if we try hard enough, we will find some useful information which we can learn from. The best leaders look for those gems rather than focus on the way the message is delivered or who it's delivered by. The key is to focus on the message, and not the messenger.

- Stay grounded on your vision and purpose: The leader's compass is their vision and their purpose. Whenever they have doubt about the direction they are headed, or receive some critical feedback, the smart leader goes back to his or her vision and key success factors. They check themselves - and the feedback - against how the issue being thought of supports or distracts from that vision. Thinking this way of the criticism puts it into context, and helps the leader determine how, or even whether, to respond.

- Get comfortable with the idea that not everyone will agree with you. Expect it and know that this is normal. I learned long ago that life – especially professional life – is not a popularity contest. When we face the reality that no one is liked by everyone, those with thick skin will not be defeated by this thought. There is simply no way that a leader will ever be liked by all the people he or she is leading. Instead, the emotionally intelligent leader focuses on taking actions that build their credibility, and demonstrate with action – more than words – that they are loyal to the vision and to their followers. The leaders that do this will be the most effective at engaging the organization to focus on achieving breakthrough results.

- Rely on your support structure. Good leaders surround themselves with great people, and they count on them to keep them grounded when critics attack. A smart leader listens to those closest to them, and seeks their advice when dealing with adversity. The smartest leaders are very careful about people who will just tell them what they want to hear, and choose instead those with the courage to tell them the truth, regardless of how tough it may be to deliver the message.

- Don't be discouraged if you fail from time to time. Understanding the root cause of failure is the seed of success in future attempts. Failure can be tough to accept. Those with thick skin use failure as fuel to ignite their imaginations and power themselves forward towards the next attempt. Failure along the way is a bump in the road and nothing more. Accepting it as an end-outcome is not at all what LegacyMan does.

There are a few watch-outs for leaders who successfully develop thick skin. Having a thick skin requires balance. If the leader develops a hard outer-shell, does not let anything get under his or her skin, and is non-emotional, they can be perceived as callous or insensitive. On the other hand, if the leader often takes things personally, or is impulsive in their response, then they may be perceived as too soft or thinned-skin, and are labeled as "being too touchy". This is typically seen as a weakness in leaders. Thus, as with most things in life, it's a game of balance. Choosing carefully the response and the measure of our response is the key in simultaneously projecting the right level of strength, humility, and sensitivity.

CHAPTER 13

LegacyWoman & LegacyMan

*L*eading is a privilege. For those who are fortunate to be bestowed that privilege, it becomes an awesome responsibility. When we lead, we are accountable to our people, our organizations, our communities, and to all whom we influence. Leading is not for the faint-hearted, or the weak-minded individual. Leadership is reserved for – indeed it demands – people of great character, strength, wisdom, compassion and drive. Perhaps now, in these times, more than any other age in history, we need great leaders to rise in all sectors – private and public - and in all parts of the world, if we as a human race are to achieve our collective potential.

We live in precarious times. We are under the constant threat of evil forces, bent on making war and inflicting terrorism.

In our world today, far too many people live in substandard conditions, and they lack basic essential and life-saving medical treatments. We lose thousands of people each year to disease for which we have yet to find cures. We are slowly destroying our natural resources to feed our inefficient infrastructures, and our insatiable appetite to consume energy. We build barriers of division and strife between people based on their religion, color or creed, rather than building the bridges that can bring us closer together towards living in a harmonious world. We can do better. We must do better. And we need leaders who will make it their purpose to enable our world to become a better place for all who inhabit it.

The solutions to our problems, across industries, sectors, governments, and communities, begin with leaders in each of these areas having a vision and mission that always aims at creating value. Whether it's in creating innovative technologies that enable us to live better lives, or technologies that save our lives – leaders can change the world. Whether they are working on creating policies and passing laws that keep the world safer for all, or support companies to effectively operate, thereby enabling industries to flourish and create jobs and wealth for the communities they serve – leaders can change the world. We need leaders in our churches, schools, small companies, large companies, our armed forces and police, our emergency responder organizations, our local government agencies, and our state and federal government agencies. We need leaders.

The skills and competencies we need in our leaders, are as varied as the many segments in which they lead. Certainly, the skills required to lead a technology or engineering firm, will be very different from those required to lead a pharmaceutical or healthcare organization. Generals in our armed forces will need different skills from the captains of industry in the oil and gas sector. Our spiritual leaders will surely have skills and qualities different than those required of civil engineering organization leaders working on urban development projects. Technical skills will be very industry specific. However, there are some traits and qualities that we require of our leaders that transcend the area in which they lead, and have everything to do with how they lead. In this book, we've explored those intrinsic values and qualities of leaders that we believe they must all possess if they are to be the most effective leaders, and if they are to live-up to their greatest potential.

In our very real world, superheroes with supernatural powers are prisoners to the universe of fiction. They don't exist. While we've had fun with the whimsical approach of analyzing these fictional characters, and creating a few new superheroes – LegacyWoman and LegacyMan – the lessons we should take away are of great consequence to real-world legacy leaders.

This author believes that out leaders - our LegacyMan and LegacyWoman - need to be more than a technical expert, financial wizard, or gifted orator. They need to possess and command the skills and traits that we explored in this book. We do want our leaders to be the amalgamation of all the finest qualities of our favorite superheroes. We want Superman, Spiderman, Wonder Woman, Iron Man, and all the others, rolled up into one. We want our leader to be a visionary, who is truthful and credible. We want a loyal leader, and one that is flexible, transparent, durable and has a fiery passion. We want an emotionally intelligent and stable leader whom we can count on when things get tough. We expect – indeed we demand – a leader who has strong will power but is not stubborn. We long for leaders who are adaptable, and can heal themselves and the team, when they are wounded. We expect our leaders to anticipate trends and issues that impact our world, and who can be innovative and breakthrough thinkers who inspire us to discover and create solutions to our problems. Importantly, we want to follow courageous leaders. Leaders who will boldly and confidently take us into uncharted waters, and navigate us through the journey of self-discovery, and who will enable us and all the people they are privileged to lead to achieve our greatest potential. LegacyWoman and LegacyMan, rise-up and lead!

Epilogue

As leaders, we don't always completely appreciate the impact that we've had on an organization and the individuals in it. The legacy we leave behind is often only understood sometime after we are no longer with the company or the group that we were privileged to lead. That may be because it's only after we are gone, that the people we've influenced, for better or for worst, talk about what we did during our tenure. Fortunately for me, as I was departing from a company that I led for some years, I was blessed to get a glimpse of the impact I had on the global team. What I experienced was a very humbling, and without doubt the most significant moment in my career as a leader. As I was transitioning the organization to my successor, I travelled with him to visit several of our facilities and regional offices. This was a very important part of completing an effective transfer of power from one leader to the next. It was also a terrific opportunity for me to say a proper farewell to the teams that I have become so fond of over the years, and for them to do the same.

Over the course of a few weeks we travelled across the globe – from California to Japan – to meet with our teams. Some were small, with just a few dozen people, and some much larger like our two manufacturing facilities each with nearly two-thousand employees. We had business meetings and conducted town-halls to talk about the transition, and to give them ample opportunity to ask questions. Importantly, it gave me the chance to introduce my successor, and demonstrate to all that this would be a smooth transition that would enable the organization to continue succeeding in the future. It was also important for me to ask them to trust him the way they had trusted me. I wanted to assure them that I felt this new leader would be loyal to them, and would support them as much as I had. What I did not expect, and was profoundly touched by, was the outpouring of emotions that came my way from them – both individually and collectively. The teams planned "going-away" dinners and celebrations, and they honored me with some incredibly meaningful words spoken during these events. They also presented me with a few gifts, all of which have great significance in their local culture, and which will forever remind me of the loyalty and trust I enjoyed while serving as their leader. Many of these mementoes now adorn my home office, and are a constant reminder of the impact that we as leaders have.

During these trips, and in our meetings with the teams, the recurring theme I heard was a deep sense of appreciation for having supported, and trusted, them. That's it! Simple. Trust and support. Of course, they mentioned how they appreciated me challenging them, and insisting that the manufacturing processes and R&D innovations were progressing. Sure, they were grateful that I provided them the resources they needed to properly get the job done. Yes, they acknowledged that I provided them with a clear vision and strategy, and that we had key success factors to guide our actions. Certainly, they appreciated my focus on organizational and people development. However, most of all, what I heard from all teams uniformly was: "thank you for supporting us and trusting us. Thank you for taking the arrows on our behalf and fighting for us individually and as a team". Their words left me nearly speechless, and always fighting to hold back tears.

On the very last day of my visit to the largest manufacturing facility, I was shocked at what they did. Nearly 1000 employees lined the entire perimeter of the manufacturing facility, and they insisted on driving me around the entire facility while standing up in the back of a pick-up truck, so that they could all wave and say farewell. I was humbled beyond words, and with tears in my eyes, I waved and smiled at each of them as they wished me well.

As we arrived back to the starting point of what could only be described as a parade, the team did something else that brought me great joy. The Master of Ceremony began to announce the arrival of some very important guests: she introduced several superheroes! As she did, members of the team, dressed in full superhero costumes, came running to the front of the podium. Then, some villains showed up and the show was on! The superheroes proceeded to defeat the bad guys, and saved the day for all! It was a short, but fun role-play, and it meant the world to me. I had presented the concept of Superhero leadership to the organization and they had taken it to heart! One of the gifts they gave me was a picture with the faces of several of my leadership team members superimposed on the bodies of the superheroes. They also superimposed my face on one of the characters – Captain America! The loyal leader! I was overwhelmed and overjoyed to know that in some small way, I made a difference.

I have never felt this way in my entire professional career, and I suspect that I never will again. I felt a deep sense of accomplishment and satisfaction; but most of all I felt a profound appreciation for having had the opportunity to impact a team in this way. I share this story not to proclaim myself a great leader. I realize that I fall short in many ways, and that my journey to becoming a true legacy leader, is a work-in-progress. Rather, I share this story as evidence that as leaders, it is unequivocal that our greatest role is to be loyal, trustworthy, credible, transparent, and visionary leaders who enable our teams to be breakthrough thinkers and inspire them to achieve their greatest potential. As leaders, we bear an awesome responsibility, but we are benefited with a sense of accomplishment that few ever enjoy. I leave you with this thought: in the immortal words of that venerable superhero of Disney's Toy Story, Buzz Lightyear: "To Infinity and Beyond".

About The Author

Anthony López is a sought-after expert on leadership and management topics. He is the author of _The Legacy Leader Series of books._ He is also the author of _"See You At The Wake: Healing Relationships Before It's Too Late"_ and _"Jag: Christian Lessons From My Golden Retriever"._

Mr. López is currently the CEO of Azzur Group, a Private Equity Medical Device and Life-Sciences services firm. He also serves as the Chairman of the Board for PROSPANICA (formerly the National Society of Hispanic MBAs). López holds a BS in Electrical Engineering, and a MS in Engineering Management. He is also a graduate of the Department of Defense Equal Opportunity Management Institute.

In 1985, López was commissioned as an Air Force Officer and served as a Flight-Test Director. He left active duty in 1991, but remained in the Air Force Reserves where he served as a Human Resources Officer until 1998. He joined Johnson & Johnson (J&J) in 1991. While at J&J he held leadership positions over an 18-year period. López also served as Chairperson for the Hispanic Organization For Leadership & Achievement (HOLA) at J&J. From 2009 to 2011, he was the Senior Vice President & General Manager for Respiratory in CareFusion – a $750 million global business. From 2011 to 2017 he served as President & General Manager at Ansell Healthcare. He is the founder of L&L Associates, A Leadership & Management Consulting group.

Mr. López is the recipient of numerous military and industry awards. His military awards include: The Meritorious Service Medal, the Air Force Commendation Medal, the Air Force Achievement Medal, the Air Defense Service Medal, and the Aerospace Primus Award. His Johnson & Johnson awards include the J&J Standards of Leadership Award, the 2006 DePuy President's Award, and the J&J Burke Award for Marketing Excellence. He is also a two-time winner of the Telly, a prestigious industry award. Tony is a 3rd Degree Black belt in the American Association of Taekwondo and a Black Belt in the International Federation of Taekwondo. He enjoys reading, writing, and physically challenging sports.

Printed in the United States
By Bookmasters